BUILD A BIGGER TABLE

Creating Space to Discuss Life & Faith

JEREMY MARTIN

outskirts
press

Outskirts Press, Inc.
http://www.outskirtspress.com

ISBN: 978-1-4787-9754-8

Outskirts Press and the "OP" logo are trademarks belonging to Outskirts Press, Inc.

PRINTED IN THE UNITED STATES OF AMERICA

Table of Contents

About Me...The Author

Who is this guy?

I'm a nobody. I promise it's true. I remember thinking when I was younger (dangerous, I know) that I wanted to be the next (_fill in the blank_) big person who did whatever it was I was interested in at the time. When I say younger, I mean well into my twenties. I'm thirty-five now.

I said this phrase one time to a man who mentored me in my youth. He looked at me with knowing eyes. I felt like I was exposed for my foolishness. He simply said, "Why don't you just worry about being the first Jeremy Martin."

What a novel idea! I hadn't considered it. Honestly.

Fast-forward to now...I'm still a nobody. But I heard recently that if you have ideas, see a problem, or want to get something out...write a book. So, that's what I'm doing. It's a slow go because I'm terrible with typing, but I'm doing it.

To help you understand who the first "Jeremy Martin" is, I want to tell you a bit about my past experiences, current situation, and future hopes and dreams.

Past Experiences

Well, to start, I was born at a very early age. This is just the beginning of corny, old-man jokes. I'm full of them.

I was born into a great family. This is not anything I did. I call that *grace*. The more I work with kids and families, the better I understand the depth of grace found in simply being born to great parents who loved each other and their kids, in that order. We had good health. We had needs met. We enjoyed most of our time together.

My dad was a well-respected man of integrity who coached basketball at our school, was a deacon in our large church, and worked his way up the right way at the only company he had ever worked for. My mom was a stay-at-home mother who lived her dream of raising children. Only she ended up helping to raise many more than the four she birthed herself. She provided a very inexpensive daycare alternative by way of our home and her love. Even to this day, she has very special relationships with children she cared for as toddlers.

I grew up going to a large, independent, fundamental Baptist church in Florida. They had a Christian school, a Bible college, a rescue mission, rehabilitation facility, summer camp, and a women and children's center. The church had boomed in the '70s and '80s, and even through a scandal in the '90s, they continued to thrive. I enjoyed my church experience.

I was active in youth group. I believed things I was told about God, the Bible, and how it all worked. This place was integral to my development as a person, pastor, and follower of Jesus.

I went to the Christian school from K-5 through twelfth grade. I even went to the Bible college for two and a half years. It seemed like the natural progression. Through a series of events I was unable to continue at that college as my family had moved to the other side of the United States. I was living alone, working two jobs, and actually growing spiritually like never before.

God tends to use rough seasons to strengthen our trust.

I did end up back in Bible college, only this time it was two semesters at a very similar church-run college in Tennessee. The best thing to come from my time there was meeting my future wife, Martha. No, she was not an elderly professor. She was a bright-eyed, super-cool, vibrant twenty-year-old point guard of the women's basketball team. I was immediately attracted to her. Not only her looks attracted me, but also her personality and vibrancy.

The next few years involved an interim role as youth director with a church in Atlanta, a move back to Florida to teach at a Christian school (a different one), and many years as a very eligible bachelor. I didn't date a lot, but I certainly did a lot of looking for a wife and not just because I felt alone, nor because I was jealous of my friends. Mainly, because in my Baptist tradition, a man wasn't fit to be a pastor until he had sealed the deal in marriage. Oh yeah, I was training to be a pastor.

It was 2009 and I was finishing up my last year of teaching. I had a degree from a Christian university, and I was on my way to Las Vegas for an internship with a church. Oh, and I was getting married before I went. Martha and I hadn't seen each other in years at this time, but marriage was a viable option. We were crazy. It was fun. She's awesome!

There's more life that happened in the next six and a half years. We moved away from Vegas after the internship to help a friend start a church in North Carolina. After that got going we realized Vegas would be our home and so we moved back to work on staff with the church where I had interned. I had the privilege of serving some great families during my time there. But something felt like I wasn't where I'd be forever.

Current Situation

In January of 2015 my wife and I decided that we would sell our home in North Las Vegas and move our family (one child and one on the way) to the Downtown District of Las Vegas. Maybe you've heard of Fremont Street. Well, we call it home now. In this revitalizing area of the city, with startup restaurants, tech companies, and businesses, we would try our hand at church "planting." I just call it a "startup church."

We have two beautiful, amazing children. Our son loves deeply and has taught my wife and me so much about seeing people the way Jesus saw them, someone created in the image of God. We rent a home we love. We are working to see our dreams come true. This book is proof. We love adventure. We love that place where fear and excitement intersect. It's where we live, figuratively, of course.

We launched Downtown Faith in January of 2017. This book is so much of what we are all about as a faith community. It's not just theory or theology. It's becoming practice and practical.

Future Hopes and Dreams

I'm excited for the unclear future that God has for us. There's so much about this journey I don't know. I had to remove one tool belt and put on a new, unfamiliar one. There's a stirring in my heart to new spiritual consciousness. I'm feeling led by God to try something new with the way this thing called the "church" operates. I'm compelled to create space for people to discuss life and faith. Even if they don't agree!

Note From The Author

Tables, Talking, Tribes, and Theology

This book is about four things that can be very powerful if understood correctly. Incorrectly, these things can and do destroy. They divide. When these things are used well, people are brought together, understood, and even transformed.

I believe the modern church must redeem tables, talking, tribes, and theology if it wants to have a place of influence within current culture.

The good news…

I'm not the only one saying these things.

These aren't new ideas; Jesus taught these clearly.

The world is ready for it.

God is big enough to handle these changes.

How to read this book

There are three attitudes to have as we approach this book: openness, humility, and practicality. This book is not a theological discourse. It's not designed to draw a hard line that things should be done a certain way. I want to start a discussion. I want to bring a perspective. My perspective.

Openness

Reading with an open mind doesn't mean you'll agree with me. As a matter of fact, I'm counting on people disagreeing. What openness does mean is we position ourselves to learn something. You might see something differently. You might grow as a person. It even means that your convictions might strengthen in the best possible way.

Feel free to disagree. Feel free to tell me why you disagree. Just don't be closed to the ideas I'm sharing.

Humility

Don't be a jerk. I could stop there, but I'll elaborate.

Part of having strong beliefs and still being able to connect with people who don't share those beliefs is to be simultaneously confident and humble.

The new journey I'm on has helped me see this truth and put it into action. I'm around people all the time who think differently than I do, not just about things like God and the Bible. There are pastors and other church people who disagree with what we are doing in Las Vegas. Even more so, they disagree with *how* we are doing it.

Through all of this, my mantra has been...*humble confidence*. I've learned to say, "I understand you think that. I could be wrong. But I'm still moving forward with what I believe."

If you approach this book with arrogance, you will find all the kindling you need to tear it and me apart. If you approach it humbly, we can disagree, love each other well, and move forward with what we believe. Give humility a try!

Practicality

As I said earlier, this isn't a theology book. We are going to look at the Bible, God, and Jesus. But the goal isn't to create a new system of theology.

It's not even a "how-to" book. It's an idea book. I have an idea. Practically, it should be read as such.

I see what I believe to be a better way to approach church strategy and meaningful discussion. I will make a few hard statements, but they will be ones of practice, not theology.

I will tell you what I believe about God in some parts, but it will be a personal statement. My general, broad strokes will be about our approach to the things we believe and how we might be able to change some stereotypes, attitudes, and conversations of those with differing opinions. I believe things can change. I don't believe this book will make them change. I just believe, practically, that a book can start a conversation.

So, read well and enjoy. And as always, join the discussion!

PART ONE

Why A Table

A single conversation across the table with a wise man is better than ten years mere study of books.
—Henry Wadsworth Longfellow

Tables are quite an interesting, yet subtle thing. They are useful. I'm sitting at one right now. Look up and around right now. Did you see a table of some sort?

Tables come in all shapes and sizes. There are hand-crafted tables made by artists, and basic tables you pieced together with instructions from Ikea. I've seen tables made from things never meant to be tables. Repurposed cable spools, doors, and boats.

Tables have been designed from wood, metal, or both. There are end tables, coffee tables, cafe/bistro tables. You'll eat this week at a restaurant or dinner table. You'll have drinks around a bar or high-top table.

Some tables have legs or bases, while others are built directly into walls or counters. Some tables are functional, while many are crafted beautifully with attention to detail and design.

So, why tables? Well, tables usually have something else. The perfect pairing. Chairs. And chairs mean people. For every table, there's a seat. The chairs come in as many shapes and sizes as the tables. From benches to couches, tables mean chairs, and chairs mean people.

We move from tables to chairs to people to something even better— energy. Something happens when people sit in chairs around tables. Whether it's a family gathering during the holidays or a night out with friends, if there's a table with chairs and people, there's bound to be an exchange of energy. And that's when stuff happens.

Ideas are born around tables. New businesses. New inventions. New friendships, trips, and tips all happen when you get tables and chairs and people and energy.

I believe Jesus understood this. I think his closest and earliest followers came to understand this. The church became energized when people were gathered at a festival and the disciples began to tell people about Jesus. Do you think there were tables at the festival? I do.

CHAPTER ONE

A Theology of Tables

Sacred Sitting, Sharing, and Snacking

There were two rooms in that Tabernacle. In the first room were a lampstand, a table, and sacred loaves of bread on the table. This room was called the Holy Place.

—Hebrews 9:2

Most people don't have a theology of tables. We don't think about tables much. And we certainly don't consider them to be holy or sacred furniture.

Sure, the "Lord's Table" at the front of the church you went to as a kid, that table was holy. Except for when you would play hide and seek around it. Or maybe you consider the big table that a priest, preacher, or pastor uses during the sermon to be holy. You know, the pulpit.

What if we looked into the Bible and the life of Jesus and the early church and began to develop a theology of tables? What if tables held more significance for people of faith? What if a theology of tables began to change the importance of tables throughout your home, community, church, and city?

Let's do that together. Let's look at tables in scripture and see if we can get more out of our tables at home. And just maybe we will consider tables at church too.

Old Testament Tables

Table of Showbread

In both the Tabernacle (tent of worship) and the Temple (house of worship) we find a very significant table. So significant it was second only to the Ark of the Covenant, in the building instructions given to Moses. These instructions were meticulous...

made of acacia wood

thirty-six inches long, eighteen inches wide, twenty-seven inches high

overlaid with gold and molded for decoration

four legs, four gold rings, and golden poles for carrying

pure gold bowls and utensils, pitchers and jars

This table was to always have bread on it. The Hebrew word translated, "showbread" literally means "bread of presence." Bread in the Old and New Testaments represents abundance and grace, or simply, abundant grace. The sole purpose of this table was to represent God's very present, abundant grace to his people. Hold on to that. It's going to take shape even more as we build our tables.

The Table of the King

There's a wonderful story in the second book of Samuel about a man named Mephibosheth. Well, it's sort of about him. It's also about a king. King David. David had a best friend, Jonathan. It's a complicated and exciting story of friendship, family, death, royalty, pursuit, marriage, and more death. But ultimately, David and Jonathan were unlikely friends (and brothers-in-law).

Some time after Jonathan died and David was king of Israel, he decided to do something kind for Jonathan's family. That's where Mephibosheth comes in. He was crippled as a small child and in that culture if you were handicapped in any way, you couldn't produce. And if you couldn't produce or reproduce, you were worthless to your family and tribe.

David decided to change this man's story. He invited him in to the heart of the kingdom. David gave him a place at the table. He commanded servants to produce for him and gifted him the land to make that happen. Look at how the author of the story puts it...

> "And from that time on, Mephibosheth ate regularly at David's table, like one of the king's own sons...And Mephibosheth, who was crippled in both feet, lived in Jerusalem and ate regularly at the king's table."

Another table. Another representation of grace. Hold on to that.

Jesus and Tables

Matthew and the Dinner Table

In a couple of the gospel accounts of Jesus' life we find a guy named Matthew (also called Levi). He was a tax collector. This was an especially hated group if you were Jewish. Tax collectors were basically economic terrorists.

They worked for the Roman Empire, collecting the taxes of the oppressed Jewish people. And they were Jewish. They would ask for a little extra in taxes and pocket the difference. The taxes were already crippling these mostly impoverished people, and now this guy comes and takes extra.

You can understand why they were hated. They were a separate class of sinner. Think of the worst of the worst in your world. That's who these people were to Jesus' people.

One day while Matthew was working in his tax collector booth (probably a table), Jesus passed by and asked him to be his follower. What?!!!? Why would he ask this guy?

Matthew said "yes" and then threw a party with Jesus as the honored guest. Who showed up? You got it. Other tax collectors and sinners. This was so scandalous that the religious elite of the day asked Jesus' disciples why Jesus would eat, presumably at a table, with "such scum."

Luke's account gives us Jesus' response to the religious elite…don't miss this.

> "Healthy people don't need a doctor—sick people do. I have come to call not those who think they are righteous, but those who know they are sinners and need to repent."

He was sitting at the table with people who understood they needed grace. Those who thought they had it all together weren't invited to the party. And worse, they couldn't understand why the party was happening in the first place.

Jesus understood that tables were about grace and parties were simply an expression of gratitude for the grace extended. Tables and chairs and people and energy and grace and food and sitting and sharing and snacking all become holy in the presence of Jesus!

Parable of the Party

Jesus liked parties and it seems he was invited often. In Luke's gospel account, we find Jesus at another feast (I bet tables were there), and everyone was scrambling to sit at the table of honor. They were all trying to get as close to the "head table" as they could.

Jesus, being Jesus, used this moment to teach about humility and invitation. It was really beautiful. He taught that the lame (I wonder if he thought of Mephibosheth), the poor, and the outcast were the ones we should be inviting to the table.

Then a guy blurted out a token religious (Christianese) statement about how good it would be to eat together at the table in the Kingdom of God. Clearly, he had just missed Jesus' point. Jesus was patient and tried again.

This time he used a parable—stories that related to common, earthly understandings of life but carried a deeper spiritual meaning by disrupting and decentering those understandings. Jesus used these a lot.

A man throws a great banquet (with tables I'm sure) and invites everyone he knows. But the RSVP situation is bleak. People are giving excuses as to why they won't be there. The man of great respect gets angry that the invited guests won't come. So, he tells his servants to go into the city and invite anyone: the lame, the poor, etc.

These people gladly accept an invitation to a banquet of such honor. But there's still room: room in the house, room at the table, room for people to sit in chairs at tables and share and snack and create enough energy to fill his house with joy. So, he sends the servants out on the roads (dangerous places in this context) to find people to join the party. He wants his house full!

There's so much in this story: the rejection of Jesus by the Jewish nation, the messianic blessing to the world found in Jesus, the reconciliation of every person to God through Jesus. Even those we don't think are "in" end up invited.

Most importantly, I think we should understand one thing. When Jesus wanted to talk about the Kingdom of God and who was going to be present, he used a banquet and tables and invitations and RSVPs to convey the point. And...we see the grace of the master of the house: grace to extend invitations, grace to open the doors, grace for new people, and no judgment for the original people...more tables, more grace.

Early Church Tables

Dinner Tables and Friends

After Jesus rose from the dead and sent his disciples out to make more disciples and "go" to the entire world with this Jesus message, we come to the book in the New Testament called Acts or The Acts of the Apostles. It's really a continuation of the gospel according to Luke. Only, the focus shifts from Jesus to the church, also known as the body of the Christ.

Here we find a man by the name of Peter rising to leadership after Jesus leaves. Jesus said this would happen. Peter preaches the message of Jesus and the church or gathering of believers and followers of Jesus begins to boom. Thousands of people at a time are joining this group. People begin seeing Jesus for who he said he was, and this changes everything.

In Acts chapter two we are given a glimpse into the natural and supernatural results of following Jesus in faith. Guess what, tables are involved. Here's how Luke described this new thing happening to the world...

"They worshiped together at the Temple each day, met in homes for the Lord's Supper, and shared their meals with great joy and generosity, all the while praising God and enjoying the goodwill of all the people."

Sounds good, right? This new community overflowed with generosity and joy and meals and meetings and breaking bread in Jesus' name, and people liked them for it. They had a good reputation. The idea that if people in your community or city hate your church you must be doing something right is wrong.

People who had received grace, extended grace generously through homes and meals and tables and chairs and praising and joy. This was a daily thing and they were liked for it. Why? People don't really have a problem with grace. Or tables. Or meals. Or joy.

Peter and the Sheet

Later on in Acts we find Peter on his roof in a "trance." How he got that way I'll leave up to you to decide. Either way, he's in a trance and sees a vision from God. The vision? A tablecloth with all kinds of animals on it.

Peter hears a voice command him to get up, kill, and eat. But Peter is Jewish. It isn't that simple. These are animals he isn't allowed to eat by law. He has never eaten these animals. Now, God is saying it's okay? Something new is happening.

Peter explains his dilemma about eating "unclean" animals. A voice responds, correcting him. He should not call things "unclean" which God calls "clean." Imagine how difficult this would be to understand. His entire life was about to change. And not just because he would get to eat bacon for the first time.

You see, according to Jewish law, there were "unclean" people as well. This perspective wasn't limited to animals and food. This was about people. This was about a bigger table with a bigger tablecloth full of the things that used to be forbidden, and people being invited. This wasn't about diet. It was about grace for a whole new people group.

How do I know? Here's what happened next.

As Peter is trying to understand what all of this means, some men show up inviting him to the house of a man named Cornelius. Cornelius was a devout man of faith in God. But he had a problem. He was a Gentile. He was "unclean." Normally, Peter would never go to the house of Gentile and certainly not *in* the house. But he just had a vision while in a trance: a vision of a tablecloth, a vision of the unclean being clean, a vision of something new. So he went.

Cornelius is ecstatic that this leader of this new movement would come *to* and *in* his house. Peter announces his prior problem with coming in as he enters. Imagine that. Walking into a guy's house and letting everyone there know you used to think they were unclean?

Peter doesn't just announce the old. He announces the new. He tells them about his vision. He shares what once was isn't any longer. A change has happened and has caused unclean people to become clean. Then he says this about his vision of a new, bigger tablecloth...

> "I see very clearly that God shows no favoritism. In every nation he accepts those who fear him and do what is right. This is the message of Good News for the people of Israel—that there is peace with God through Jesus Christ, who is Lord of all."

Don't miss it. God showing "no favoritism" is God showing grace. And how did God communicate to Peter that his grace was for everyone?

A tablecloth with pre-food. God accepts. There's peace in and through Jesus. New invitations to new people for a new life.

Peter was beginning to build a bigger table!

Last Thoughts on Theology and Tables

These examples are by no means the full extent of tables in the Bible. We'll get to more throughout this book. But I do think these examples compel us to consider a theology of tables.

These stories should move us to consider our table—our current table—and to ask ourselves questions about our table(s).

> How big is my table?
>
> How welcoming is my table?
>
> How am I using my table?
>
> Am I at the table of the King?
>
> Who's at my table?
>
> Who's not at my table?
>
> What's preventing people from being at my table?

These are just a few questions we should be asking. It's a great place to start. If we are going to build a bigger table, we must become aware of our current views of what the table even is, and allow God to open our hearts and minds to the possibility of a brand-new perspective. One that includes more people sitting in more chairs having meaning-ful conversation around a bigger table!

CHAPTER TWO

Building Tables at Church

Four Spiritual Experiences

> *Theologically and objectively speaking, we are already*
> *in union with God. But it is very hard for people to believe or*
> *experience this when they have no positive sense of identity,*
> *little courage yet, no strong boundaries to contain Mystery,*
> *and little inner religious experience at any depth.*
>
> —Richard Rohr, *Falling Upward*

We've been doing this church startup thing for a few months now. Building a bigger table is at the heart of our mission and strategy. We sit around tables. We believe there's something theological about it. On a deeper level, we've discovered something spiritual about it too.

It's good to be theological; it's better to be spiritual and to be rooted in your image and identity coming directly from the Divine. Spirituality takes us places theology cannot. While one builds the intellect, the other builds relationships.

I can know all of the right things about my wife and still not love her deeply. The same is true of God and people. I can know everything

Jesus meant when he said to love God with every part of our being and love our neighbor as ourselves. But it doesn't mean that I will experience either of those two things fully.

There's a unique spiritual progression happening around tables when we create space to discuss life and faith. I'd like to share those with you before moving on to the nuts and bolts of building your table. For us, these things are becoming the key to engaging people in meaningful discussion around tables. We're also seeing people experience spiritual awakening through these God-conversations.

Communion, Connection, Community, Continuity

The Lord's Table

Whether you call it The Lord's Supper, The Lord's Table, Communion, Eucharist, or something else, central to following Jesus is the beautiful remembrance taking place as we break bread and drink wine (or juice) together. But it's more than this. Communion is about joining an already existing, active, creative energy.

I like to call it Dynamic Communal Energy. Catchy, right?

Early in the Bible we find out something about this creative, divine source of all of existence. It's communal. Strange, right? This singular being is somehow also living in eternal, infinite communion with itself. Check out how the author of Genesis tells the story of the creation of humanity...

> Then God said, "Let us make human beings in our image, to be like us."

God, singular, said, "let us," plural, do something; create, create humans. These humans, or "adams" in the Hebrew, would be "like us," God says. This is so interesting on many levels. Let's explore a few together.

First, God was creating and giving purpose to everything. It's not just what God was doing. It's who God is. And humans would be like this: active, creative, working with purpose. They would be given responsibility. Human beings were created then invited into the creative work of God on Planet Earth. That's pretty cool.

Next, we see that God is communal by nature and humans would be made like that too. Our very spirit craves communion. Not just with God, but with everyone and everything. One way to view sin is simply the detaching of humanity from God and each other. We are designed to share: to share life and purpose, to share with and in the Divine source of all life.

Are you starting to see how communion is more than some bread and wine? It's bigger than your church, your tribe, or your doctrinal stance on communion. It's about engaging our life with the Source of life: sharing life, celebrating life together, with others.

God's invitation to the world is for relational transformation, not religious transaction. It's about rejoining this Dynamic Communal Energy in the work of redeeming and restoring the world. We are welcomed back into relational change for God's glory and our good.

God invites us to the table and to build a bigger table!

As Jesus sat with his disciples just hours before he would be arrested and crucified he told them this...

> "...just as my Father has granted me a Kingdom, I now grant you the right to eat and drink at my table in my Kingdom."

Jesus was inviting them into his Kingdom; a kingdom where Jesus is King. A kingdom built on things like love and sacrifice, not violence and power. He invited them to the table. The table of the King. And they would be tasked with inviting others to the table of the King.

And you know who was sitting at this literal, physical table, being invited to this deeply spiritual table? Peter, who would one day stand in front of a man named Cornelius and share Jesus' invitation to sit at the table and build a bigger table.

By definition communion is the sharing or exchanging of intimate thoughts and feelings between friends, especially when the exchange is on a mental or spiritual level. As followers of Jesus, we participate in ceremony called communion, the celebration and contemplation of friendship with God through Jesus.

But I hope now we see communion as so much more: as partnership with the very Creator of the universe who loves us and wants us and is for us. Oh, and for them too!

At the Table with Others

The next step in this deeply spiritual progression around the table is *connection*. While communion involves our participation with God, connection develops when we participate with others. This participation involves listening and sharing, usually around a table.

Brené Brown, author of *Daring Greatly* and several other amazing books about living life in a meaningful way, describes it this way...

> "Connection is the energy that is created between people when they feel seen, heard, and valued; when they can give and receive without judgment."

Does this sound like a gathering at your church? How about the church down the road? What about the church in which you grew up? Probably not. On rare occasions, this type of connection is experienced between followers of Jesus, but seldom is that depth of relationship felt throughout the body of the church.

Like so many other places in life and society, the church can be without true care and compassion. There's little space designed to be our true self; a space created specifically for people to wrestle with life's struggles while surrounded by non-judgmental listening.

I believe the best way to become new is by connecting with others who are committed to becoming new.

This doesn't happen in rows. It happens around tables. Think of the last hard conversation you had to have with a friend or loved one. What was the environment? Was it a classroom with a whiteboard and a podium? Did you take them to a concert? Probably not. It was probably at the dinner table. Or you may have had them sit on a couch next to you as your coffee mugs rested on the table in the center of the room.

Are you getting my point? Maybe the very way in which our churches are designed to look and feel and accommodate is the very thing keeping us from true, spiritual connection with God and others. Remember the early church? Remember how they met? What if we got back to that? What if we really connected with each other?

A Community Table

Once you've begun to experience continuous communion and con-nection, this other thing begins to happen to you, your church, and your surrounding neighborhoods. Community starts to take hold and bring you all together. I'm not talking about functional church com-munity. I'm talking about people inside and outside of the community of faith, truly living life together.

All of a sudden, it doesn't matter as much who does or doesn't believe like you. It only matters who's there and who's not. Who's there, so they can be known and cared for, and who's not, so they can be invited. We've already established that the natural result of faith is community. Remember the church in Acts?

This isn't just any community, mind you. It's a community that makes its larger community better. It is a community of faith that the surrounding communities have faith in. People not yet a part of the faith begin to look in, walk in, and jump in to participate with a whole new community because they see this gathering and its tables as *for* them!

It's at this level that the city and the church begin to make each other better. The tables become more diverse. Sure, people of all kinds are sitting at the Table of Jesus within the church, but now the people of the church are sitting at tables in and around the city. Tables where decisions are being made. Tables of people who are creating, innovat-ing, and building within the city. This is community and it begins and ends at tables.

A Unified Table

Unity is tricky. We don't see it a lot. Teams have inner division through competition. Companies lose people through new ideas or changing policy. Should I even mention our government and party politics? Unity is elusive.

Continuity is even more difficult an aspiration. The idea of a continuous or connected whole seems impossible. At some level dissension happens and seems inevitable. Certainly this is true of the church as a whole and almost any local church you find.

It just seems unlikely that any gathering of people can truly be so unified they create a meaningful organization able to maintain continuity throughout its existence. I've been in enough churches to be skeptical. I've seen good people treating others badly, leaders consumed with pride and self-elevation, and narrowing theology pushing people out and away from the table of God.

The growing diversity in our country and its cities makes this even more difficult. We tend to like people who are like us. With everyone else, it just seems too difficult. There's nowhere we need more unity in the midst of diversity than within the church. Is there any hope?

I think so.

The Apostle Paul, church entrepreneur and missionary extraordinaire, gives us the ingredients to make this happen. It's a simple recipe. Not easy, mind you, just simple. He cites Jesus as our reference point.

In his letter to the church at Philippi, Paul urges them toward unity this way...

"You must have the same attitude that Christ Jesus had.

Though he was God, he did not think of equality with God as something to cling to.
Instead, he gave up his divine privileges, he took the humble position of a slave and was born as a human being. When he appeared in human form, he humbled himself in obedience to God and died a criminal's death on a cross."

Did you catch the ingredients?

The four ingredients to achieve continuity in the church (and around the church) are as follows: humility >>> sacrifice >>> love >>> unity. Unity requires love, and love always includes sacrifice. And no one sacrifices without first humbling themselves.

We will get more into this later. We are going to see humility as the lynchpin to building bigger tables, with Jesus as our greatest instructor and example. Humility around tables can change everything. I'm not going to lie. Around the table, discussing important matters, might be the most difficult place to find and/or muster humility.

Remember, the table isn't just theological, it's spiritual. That's good news. It's our spirit that connects with the Spirit of God to show us our relationship. It's in our spirit that we can truly commune and connect with God and others. Tables are spiritual. More so than we've realized in our simple, human understanding. But that's changing. We're changing. Can you feel it?

Something is opening up. It's chairs around your table!

CHAPTER THREE

All Are Welcome, Even Jesus

There's A Chair

I sat back, enjoying my extra special bitter ale and listening to the discussion going on around me. I thought, this is what it's all about: people of diverse backgrounds, experiences, and religious perspectives all sitting at the same table, having a rich, meaningful, and respectful conversation, even as differences of opinions are voiced.

—*Bryan Berghoef,* Pub Theology: Beer, Conversation, and God

If we cannot tell yet, God is inviting everyone to the table. Jesus makes a special point to highlight the invitation from God to those we might never imagine are invited. Peter had his entire first understanding of who's in and who's out shaken by God. He couldn't help but see the table as opened to everyone.

This is difficult. Honestly. We love binary thinking and in many ways this serves us well. Knowing where we belong, and to whom, helps us adapt socially. But those necessary, early ways of thinking can keep us from growing up and out into a bigger, brighter view of the gospel.

The gospel is simply the announcement that Jesus has won. Defeated sin. Grace now rules, not sin. But far too often, it is the very people who say they believe this who reject grace, at least in part. The idea that grace is for me is exciting. The idea that it's for them too is not. Somehow, we believe grace is diminished the more it's distributed. That's not how it works.

Grace is for the oppressed and the oppressor. For those in my "tribe" and those outside. We minimize the grace of God and silence the gospel announcement when we believe neither can be freely given nor broadly accepted.

Maybe you think viewing an open gospel belittles sin and brokenness. I assure you it cannot. It simply acknowledges the great victory of Jesus to overcome sin and restore all things to himself. Opening the grace and gospel of Jesus to the world is a necessary step in building a bigger table.

Let's get into this a little more and examine the many ways we close the table of God, and make it so small Jesus might not even be able to fit.

Making Room for Jesus

The table is the Lord's. I don't want to confuse anyone. Jesus built the table. God sent the invites. It's God's Kingdom and Jesus is King. That's *the* table. What I want to look at closely is your table: the table you've created, the one you're inviting people to. Maybe it's the table at your church. People have helped you build this table. It's small. Not a lot of room for the "other."

Does this table have enough room for Jesus?

You may say, "My table only has room for Jesus!" That sounds fine but it doesn't play out. Time and again we find Jesus with the other, the outcast, and the oppressed. If he's over there with them, maybe he's not really at your table.

This is the problem the religious elite had with Jesus. They couldn't believe that he would sit and eat with those people. The prostitute, the tax collector, Zaccheaus, Mary Magdalene, the blind, the leper, and others. How could a "holy" person spend so much time with the unholy and unclean?

Think of our culture and society. Think of your friends and your church. Who do you consider the tax collector of your day...the Muslim down the street? Who do you see as the leper...your gay uncle? Do you see anyone as unredeemable? Who is your "other"?

If you can't make room for them at your table, then Jesus isn't sitting at your table. There's not enough room for you and yours at such a small table. Here's how Jesus said it...

> "Then they will reply, 'Lord, when did we ever see you hungry or thirsty or a stranger or naked or sick or in prison, and not help you?'
>
> "And he will answer, 'I tell you the truth, when you refused to help the least of these my brothers and sisters, you were refusing to help me.'"

Think about what Jesus is saying here. If you cannot accept the marginalized at your table, you cannot and will not accept him. We all like to think we're on "team Jesus," but ultimately the things we've leaned on to get us "in" might be the very things that have kept us out.

BUILD A BIGGER TABLE

Dining, Not Doctrine

Legend has it that on the morning of October 31, 1517, a humble monk by the name of Martin Luther nailed his "95 Theses" to the door of the Wittenberg Castle Church. This document questioned current church teachings and proposed reformed teaching, primarily that salvation was by grace through faith and not through the purchase of indulgences.

This, along with widespread availability of translated scriptures and early church writings from the likes of Augustine, sparked the Protestant Reformation. As this movement expanded, so did the ability to read and interpret biblical writings. Church leaders of all kinds debated, discussed, and even died over disagreements about church and biblical doctrine.

Defining Doctrine

A simple dictionary definition of doctrine reads as follows: a body or system of teachings related to a particular subject.

Certainly, churches and religions contain doctrine, but areas of study such as science, politics, and philosophy all have their principles, positions, and policies they advocate for and teach collectively. Doctrine is everywhere and it is educating.

Doctrine involves all kinds of information that shapes our thoughts and our thinking. No area of academia is immune to doctrine. Every field teaches prescribed truth and even systematizes their lessons to help students memorize and understand the information they consider to be the highest, most current truth on the matter at hand. We've all been exposed to doctrine, espouse doctrine, and engage in doctrinal discussions throughout our daily interactions.

I think you're starting to get my point. You may think doctrine is only for church people. Others have it to. You've had your mind shaped and are continually having it shaped anew. You hold to certain matters as truth and probably even argue your side. I mean, just peruse Facebook for a bit and you'll see everyone's doctrine splattered about in forms of memes, videos, and "this person destroys this group's argument" posts.

It's all doctrine!

Good Doctrine

The best thing about doctrine is how it instructs people with a very systematic approach designed to grow students in knowledge and practice. From science to religion this systematic approach moves learners from one thing to the next.

Doctrine often targets the next generation in hopes that they will carry it into the future and maybe even expand their tribe's understanding of how these teachings impact the world around them. Many times this is called indoctrination. And that sounds like a bad thing...especially if someone is indoctrinated into something you think is wrong.

But of course, people are fully content to indoctrinate people into their way of thinking. We think we are right, here's our proof, and this is how you regurgitate our system. Sound familiar? Of course. You fall into some category; democrat/republican, atheist/theist, evolutionist/intelligent designist (if that's even how you say it), attachment parent/baby wiser, etc. Just fill in your category and tell me who you are opposed to!

Doctrine is good because it gives your tribe a legacy of learning to pass on to the next generation and convert new believers/thinkers to your system of truth.

But doctrine can be a horrible weapon used to divide, ostracize, and belittle those who espouse a differing truth.

When doctrine becomes dangerous

A group of upset middle school students burst through my classroom door one afternoon just before seventh period. One was visibly sad while the others were angry. In case you aren't familiar with middle schoolers, they can get pretty emotional. I assumed someone said something mean about a friend, or maybe some tense "dating" issues had erupted. I was wrong...

"Mr. Martin [as I was known to the students], Miss [insert fictitious teacher name] just said that [insert fictitious student name]'s uncle who's sick in the hospital will probably die and go to hell and God wants it that way!"

Okay...serious. Being a committed faculty member, I didn't want to assume this was true. Heck, being human, I didn't want to assume this was true. This was a private Christian school and we taught the Bible and Jesus and God's love. This sounded hateful.

I did what any good faculty member does when approached with a situation like this—pass it up to the administration and wash my hands of it. Unfortunately, as the chaplain of the school, it just fell right back into my lap. I had to have the tough conversation. It's part of leadership.

After school, I headed to said teacher's room. She taught math. She was young, articulate, experienced, and a little intimidating. She had a permanent scowl, even when she smiled. I think there's a name for that kind of face nowadays, but I digress.

I sat down in the front row and quickly began by assuring her that I understand how students exaggerate. This is especially true when it comes to something a math teacher said. Then I explained what I heard. She responded, "That's exactly what I said!"

Yeah, I know. Lump in the throat. Stammering. Trying to catch up in my mind. This couldn't be true. She was so cold. She had been cruel and now brazenly admitted her cruelty. Maybe you read this and you think, "Well, she told the truth." Maybe that's what you would've said to this young student. And maybe you would hide behind the Bible like she attempted to do.

I won't go into the entire conversation but ultimately it ended with…

"Okay. Well, I promise not to teach math in my Bible class as long as you promise not to teach the Bible in your math class."

This interaction was only the beginning of many other interactions where people who followed Jesus, the teacher on love, used the Bible, the words of Jesus, and theology as a weapon to hurt people in the name of "doctrine."

I want to be clear, I'm not even saying that everything they believed is necessarily, inherently wrong. But they took something beautiful and made it an ugly, violent weapon. And these people are not the original weaponizers of their faith. Religion and irreligion have a history of hate, violence, and harshness with words. All in the name of "doctrine."

Weaponizing Belief

I think we can all agree, when a person's belief system leads them to hurt others with words or actions, faith becomes dangerous. I think more and more people are disengaging from their faith because it has at some point become harsh or even violent.

When we think of "extremism" in religious circles, it's easy to point fingers at Muslim terrorists or Westboro Baptist Church protestors. But it's not just extremist views of religion that harm people. Again, you can have correct doctrine and still use it to mistreat people.

In our culture, we've believed the lie that it's a good thing to be tolerant as long as it's with other tolerant people. But as soon as a group becomes viewed as intolerant, they are fair game to abuse with words and possibly actions. This thinking leads to hypocrisy and irrational behavior.

I've even recently been berated on social media for believing the very thing in this book, the idea that we all have faith. Some very judgmental, irrational, hate-filled things were written and posted about me. It was so weird because these were the same people who would cry foul the moment a Christian opposed same-sex marriage or a Muslim refused basic rights to a woman.

There's one basic reason why doctrine, belief, and faith become a weapon in the hands of humans who start out meaning well…passion!

A passion for truth or right.

A passion for their tribe or circle.

A passion for their family and friends.

A passion for their field of study.

A passion for their way of existing.

Passion fuels the weaponization of faith. In our attempt to be right and certain, we inadvertently become hateful and derogatory. The tighter we hold to something, the harder we grip our truth, the more evident our fists become to those around us. And when challenged, we cannot help but hurl our ideals at someone's face.

There's a lot of intellectually secure Christians out there. They know the right things to say. They've read the verses. There's not a pastor preaching something they haven't heard and studied. They're the smartest at the table and this has been their security blanket time after time. But what if that doesn't really matter?

What if communing with Jesus is more about dining than doctrine?

We like systems. They put things in their place. They help us decide who's in our tribe, our camp, and who's not. We like these clearly drawn lines in the sand. It's not that people won't admit they have more to learn. It's that everything they can learn about God will fit into a pre-made box. This feels good.

I understand this feeling. But I'm also understanding the excitement and beauty of taking a spiritual sledgehammer to your boxes. The wonder of opening your heart and mind to new thinkers, thinking about old things in refreshing ways. I'm experiencing the joy found when someone from a religious group you'd never associate with crowds your mind with their understanding of Jesus, the Bible, or God.

They're out there, and they are dining with God. Truly communing deeply. Jesus is at their table and they're learning from him how to love the "other" and the outcast like never before. I literally have chills as I type these words. I've found them. Authors and priests and philosophers who've partnered with God in my transformation. I'm loving God and following Jesus better because I've opened my heart and mind to new. My table is bigger. And I'm better for it.

Open Table

My first job was as a host for Red Lobster. This was slightly stressful. When people are hungry, they want a table. They get pushy. They are looking out for themselves. They want a table, a seat. On especially busy days it can be crazy at the host stand in a restaurant like that.

Then it happens. The family next in line sees it. An open table just their size. I've seen people just walk up and take it even before it gets cleaned. They don't care. They just want a table and this one is open!

It's interesting to think about this in spiritual terms. Jesus has an open table. People love an open table. It means it's their time to sit and eat.

I think one of the biggest obstacles to people following Jesus is the perceived closing of the table by churches and Christians. If someone doesn't feel they "fit" at a table, that table isn't for them. We've misrepresented the table of Jesus for far too long.

The rest of this book is going to be my attempt to help churches and Christians build bigger tables and open up some chairs. I want to help people follow Jesus. We will remove obstacles keeping the world at bay and find ways to be better at being a church for our community.

It's as easy as being open. But that's harder than we think. Even now I imagine the discomfort you're experiencing, thinking of inviting all kinds of people to the table.

Here we go…let's get to building!

PART TWO

Shaping the Tabletop

Eating is so intimate. It's very sensual.
When you invite someone to sit at your table and
you want to cook for them, you're inviting a person into your life.

—Maya Angelou

The first and most difficult thing we must do is decide the shape, size, texture, and scope of our tabletop. This is where the bread and wine will sit. This is where the sound of our stories will reverberate as we share and listen. This is where our elbows will rest as we lean in to the "other," and where our heads will lay as we struggle with the pain of community.

The top of the table gets the scratches, the dents, the gouges. It's where the kids will bang and the board games are played. It's seen more than the legs or the chairs. It's how we know where the table is as we find a place to sit. We point to the tabletop as we invite our guests to sit, eat, and discuss.

We must craft this tabletop to endure. We must shape it to expand. We must make it beautiful and welcoming.

So, what exactly is our tabletop?

It's probably more, but I think we should examine two things in particular that Jesus was masterful at handling, yet two things we've made a mess of as his church. First, tension. We don't walk well in tension. Jesus models this balance throughout his ministry. We have a lot to learn. Tension rests on the top of the table. It's created when diversity sits down and disagreements begin.

Next, we must address our words and the heart from which they flow. Our mouths are like water faucets. It's where the water comes out but not where it rests. The hearts of Jesus followers must mirror the heart of Jesus, or we lose the credibility to even speak the words we must.

These next few chapters will not be easy to process for some. For others, they will affirm your current frustrations. I can say, when I settled on living within the tensions of spirituality, life got more difficult. It also got bigger, brighter, fuller, and more meaningful.

CHAPTER FOUR

Embrace the Tension

Existing Within the Messy In-Between

We who in engage in nonviolent direct action are not the creators of tension.
We merely bring to the surface the hidden tension that is already alive.

—Martin Luther King, Jr.

High-Wire Act

Early one New York morning, as the fog dissipated and the sun broke through the horizon, something paused the busy city streets. Crowds gathered and looked up under the shadow of the World Trade Center, Twin Towers. "Man on wire," rang out on the police scanners. Philippe Petit was 110 stories high, balancing on a cable that had been stretched diagonally between the two enormous towers. He walked back and forth between the buildings. He kneeled and acknowledged the roars from the crowds below. At one point, he even laid down on the wire in blessed rest and pure enjoyment.

For Philippe, the wire meant escape. It meant truly living. It meant no one could touch him. Police awaited him on either building as helicopters circled above. And yet he walked. This "man on wire" relished the tension of his cable and embraced the danger of his walk. For him, life was only really lived while in between.

"There is no why," he said in the documentary, *Man on Wire*. "To me, it's, it's really, it's so simple, that life should be lived on the edge of life. You have to exercise rebellion, to refuse to tape yourself to rules, to refuse your own success, to refuse to repeat yourself, to see every day, every year, every, every idea as a, as a true challenge, and then you are going to live your life on a tightrope."

Funambulism is the literal walking of a tightrope, and Philippe Petit is probably the most famous funambulist of all time. His late-night break-in of the WTC buildings was nothing short of criminal and awesome. But this adventure is more than just a story of daring escapades. It's a lesson about tension. It's about truly living, and not just living and dying. It is a metaphor for the funambulism of life and how a full life is lived somewhere between two opposing dogmatic statements.

We get more out of life when we embrace and engage the tension!

What is tension?

Trust me when I say I understand the negativity around a word like tension. We spend a lot of time and money relieving ourselves of tension. From counseling to vacation, from comfortable beds to therapeutic massages, we want to rid ourselves of tension, not embrace it. But what if we defined tension a bit differently? What if there's more to it? What if we could begin to get comfortable with the discomfort of tension?

First, let's define tension. Literally, tension is the state of being stretched. Emotionally and/or mentally, we understand that the state of stretching causes strain, and strain is bad. Or is it? Stress and strain do have benefits. Stretching muscles before and after a workout helps your body condition itself. Strain on coal produces diamonds. And distressed jeans are back in style. Okay, maybe that was a stretch. Pun intended.

What do we mean by tension?

We all understand tension and why we wouldn't want to live in that state. We all get that walking on a high wire like Petit is dangerous, frightening, and illegal. We don't want to embrace that kind of life. But maybe if we shift our perspective a bit, we can learn to engage with tension in a productive, beneficial way. In a way that makes us and the world around us come alive with excitement. We love great stories, but we rarely welcome the pain associated with true adventure.

Tension exists. To deny it gives it power. To engage with it gives us the power to create lasting change.

So, what do we mean by tension?

Simply put, the messy in-between.

Somewhere in between…

> *the real and the ideal.*
> *grace and truth.*
> *what we know to be true and what we hope to be true.*
> *certainty and uncertainty.*
> *feeling and principle.*
> *the spiritual and the physical.*

We tend to stand on one side or the other while someone else does the same. Living life this way keeps us at a distance from people and makes viewing them as the "other" comfortable and accepted. We tribe up and stay away. Stepping out onto the tightrope, the tension, means taking a step toward someone else and their worldview. Embracing the tension doesn't mean embracing an opposing view, but it could mean embracing another person.

And that's how Jesus lived, died, and lived again!

Grace & Truth

Jesus stirred the waters and was eventually killed in the most scandalous fashion because he embraced and engaged with tension so much so that his closest followers described him as the very embodiment of grace and truth.

> "The Word became flesh
> and took up residence among us.
> We observed His glory,
> the glory as the One and Only Son from the Father,
> *full of grace and truth.*" (emphasis mine) — Apostle John

Truth says, "You're wrong, I'm right."

Grace says, "It doesn't matter who's right or wrong. Here's love, acceptance, and forgiveness."

Existing too much on either side causes some real problems. Some of us are TRUTH people and others are GRACE people. But standing on a side, and only that side, produces a mindset that just doesn't work. Let me explain it like this...

TRUTH-only people tend to be judgmental, legalistic, harsh, inflexible enforcers. Maybe you know a Christian like this. Maybe you've had a boss like this. Maybe you're like this. Either way, this person is hard to be around and, quite frankly, no fun.

GRACE-only people tend to be open, whimsical, generous, loving, flexible victims. Maybe you know a Christian like this. Maybe you've had a professor like this. Maybe you're like this. Either way, this person can be exhausting and a bit unbalanced.

You see, any time we exist on only one side, we can be very dogmatic but not very realistic. We can believe no one should be judged, but then someone rapes or murders a loved one and we want judgment. We can believe that certain truths are inflexible; then we learn the world isn't flat and we have to bend to new discovery.

Our arguments for a particular viewpoint will eventually come to a place that even we contradict.

I believe that Jesus embodied grace and truth so that he could be complete and without contradiction in the face of real life. Jesus understood it was about the real *and* the ideal, not the real *versus* the ideal. Here are a few examples of how Jesus showed us how to embrace the "and" and not the "or."

Embodiment in Jesus

Story number one…

Jesus was walking with his disciples and they came to a town called Samaria. Jesus and his followers were Jewish, which meant they were supposed to hate and avoid the people living in this town of Samaritans. This town was full of people who were bred out of a specific breaking of Jewish law. This made them unclean. And that made them reviled and hated by the "pure" Hebrew people.

Normally, Jewish people would walk approximately fifty miles out of the way to avoid going through this town. Instead, Jesus stopped by a well and commanded his disciples to go into the town and get food. This was counter-cultural and borderline damning to Jesus and his disciples.

While his followers went into the town Jesus waited by the well. Eventually a woman came to the well. She came later than the normal time. Many believe this is because she was an outcast and ostracized by her community, meaning, she was the lowest of the low. Not to mention she was a woman. Culturally, women were regarded mostly as possessions and held little to no status. The lowest of the lowest of the low approached Jesus at the well.

Jesus shocked her and the world by speaking to her. He started the discussion. This "religious leader" stepped onto the wire and in the direction of this "sinner." Through discernment and humility, Jesus discussed life and faith with this very broken woman. He spoke of her misunderstandings of God. He addressed her promiscuous lifestyle. Then he offered her life, real life, true living based on relationship to him.

In grace, Jesus shows love and kindness while never excusing or enabling. Jesus walks the wire. He embraces the "and." He changes a life and a city. A life and a city so "messy," the TRUTH-only people would avoid it at all cost.

Story number two...

Jesus took his followers up on a mountain, sat down, and began to teach. This was his most famous "sermon" ever, The Sermon on the

Mount. This teaching was really the core teaching of Jesus. He spoke of everything from loving your enemies to divorce. He truly gave the "ideal" way to live life. And it was some hard teaching, without a ton of grace.

The people he addressed really knew the law. They had learned it from as early as they could remember. They had parents and teachers helping them know how not to break God's law. They even had laws around the actual laws so as not to fall into sin. Sound familiar?

As Jesus addressed several specific laws like adultery, murder, and lying, he did something unusual. He taught these fairly straightforward laws with a bit of a twist. "You've heard it said but I say."

Jesus got to the heart of the matter and began to add the intent of the law to the letter of the law. This may have seemed harsh at the time. And it was. He took murder from a physical act to an intent of the heart. He claimed that even wanting someone dead meant murder was in your heart. He took lust from a harmless mental exercise to adultery in your heart.

In truth, Jesus got to the very heart of the listeners. It gets to our heart as well. We can view things as harmless and trivial but in reality, the truth is they hold deep significance in how we interact with people. Jesus tackled a subject that GRACE-only people avoided, because it felt uncomfortable.

Story number three...

Religious leaders had caught a woman in adultery, one of the things Jesus railed against in his sermon, and threw her at his feet. I've always wondered where the man was in this scenario. It takes two to tango, and to have sex. But the leaders only arrested the woman. She was caught, and now publicly humiliated. They asked Jesus what he would do.

Jesus knew the law. He had expanded the law with authority. He had every legal right to stone her as the law commanded. They had every right to kill her where she lay as an example to all others. So they asked Jesus what he would do.

Jesus sort of ignored them and began to write something in the dirt. We aren't told what it is, but the religious leaders demanded a response. He stood and said, "All right, but let the one who has never sinned throw the first stone!" Then he got back down and began to write in the dust again.

The storyteller tells us that the men began to walk away one by one, the oldest to the youngest. Soon Jesus was left standing alone with the woman. He asked where her accusers had gone, and if anyone had condemned her. She said no, with relief, I'm sure. Then Jesus said something powerful. He put the "and" to work and engaged the tension of this messy situation.

"Neither do I condemn you; go, and from now on sin no more."

In GRACE and TRUTH, Jesus forgave the woman and encouraged her to stop sinning. He refused to condemn her to the penalty of the law, while also acknowledging that she was in the wrong. He loved her and corrected her in the same sentence.

Jesus did the most difficult thing imaginable and walked the wire between grace and truth like a spiritual funambulist!

The "And" Matters

If the word "tension" stresses you out, then think of this idea as simply embracing the "and" in life.

We live in a very binary world where "or" is much more comfortable than "and." We get "or." It eliminates thinking. "Or" puts us in a place and keeps us safely entrenched in familiarity. "And" messes things up. It confuses comfortability. "And" means things get muddy, murky, and unclear. "And" messes with our theories and articulations. "And" makes things like politics, religion, and science less black and white and a little more gray.

The "and" matters though. It allows us to build relationships, expand our thinking, and if nothing else, soften our tone and approach to discussions about meaningful things. It allows us to hold our beliefs while also understanding that someone else believes differently and we could both be wrong.

The "and" matters because ultimately it's where real life is lived, interpreted, and translated. If a kid grows up being told one thing is the only true thing and later learns something else is true too, or at least that someone else thinks it is, everything they thought they knew about life comes into question. This really shakes people. This really hurts people.

A Christian leader I really admire, Reggie Joiner, once said this about tension...

"Tension doesn't make truth less true, it makes it more real."

We worry that "and" in our world means we don't really believe what we believe. And if your career, heaven and hell, or money is on the line, you are even more likely to run from "and." If our life and/or livelihood is built on our dogmatic statements made in the classroom, pulpit, or best-selling books, "or" is a friend and "and" could destroy everything.

What if we embraced the "and"? Could that open doors to new experiences and relationships? Could that give us more influence and not less?

The Real and the Ideal

Honestly, this is the tension hurting people most, especially when it comes to following Jesus, believing in a God, and trusting a religious system. People hear all about the ideal when they sit in church but live in the real the rest of the week and cannot reconcile the differences. Many times, what's said on Sunday doesn't help what's experienced on Monday. And that's a real problem. When the church cannot connect God's ideal to people's real in a loving way, they tend to move in a different, more relatable direction.

Safety is found in places that acknowledge the real. Security is experienced with people who authentically discuss the real. Ideal is hard, unrealistic, and discouraging.

Think of that man who has strong biblical beliefs about marriage being forever. But at home his marriage is in shambles and he just can't do it anymore. His ideal and his real are in conflict. Because his real is more tangible, attainable, and safe, he divorces his wife and leaves the church.

Think of the high school kid who loses a parent. At church, they tell her to trust God. Don't question things. Have more faith. But she leaves for college and there are other people saying different things. They introduce her to things that will numb the pain. No trusting necessary. These things are real and they can really help the pain. So, she drinks a lot and leaves the church. Drinking with these friends becomes more secure than hiding pain with the church.

I think it's important that the church learns to embrace the "and" and engage the real with the ideal on things like (*not original; material from Reggie Joiner talk at Orange Conference 2014*):

You can know God — God is a mystery

You can follow Jesus in a moment — It takes a lifetime to discover what that means

The Bible is all true — Not all truth is found in the Bible

Trust leads to stronger faith — Doubt leads to stronger faith

God has an ideal for things like marriage, sex, family — God uses broken people

Church should be enjoyed — The world should be enjoyed

Belief matters — People matter more

Just for fun I've put together a list for my irreligious, atheist, and un-churched friends. I think these apply in the same way…

Science leads to understanding — Science doesn't understand everything

The material world is to be seen and believed — Some things seen and believed are spiritual

Religion and the religious are inconsistent — People are inconsistent; including me

Education is important — Academics doesn't necessarily mean intelligence

People should just be kind to everyone and let them be whoever they want to be — People of all kinds are unkind and we can't let rapists be who they want to be

I'm sure these lists aren't entirely applicable or complete, but I think they help us think a little further about how we live in the "and."

Again, I believe life is best lived in between two opposing dogmatic statements. It's a place of balance and understanding. It's a place of true vitality. It's a difficult place to exist. It's full of unknowns, mess, and stretching. But stretching is healthy.

3 Quick Lessons

Thinking back to our opening illustration of Philippe Petit and his team, I have a few suggestions for anyone desiring to step out onto the tension. Sadly, it doesn't just happen. It isn't the easy thing to do. Embracing and engaging tension isn't natural or normal. We must work to learn how and practice daily.

It Takes Passion

The first lesson learned from reading and studying the daring acts of the French funambulist is...

It takes passion to embrace and engage the tension.

There's something special about a person with passion. The very idea is that they hurt for their goals and loves. We will never step out and create space for meaningful discourse with "the other" unless we develop a passion. It might be a passion for others. It might be a passion for discourse. Maybe, it will even be a passion for humble learning.

It doesn't matter where the passion comes from, but it does have to be present. Without passion, we will quit when it gets difficult. Without passion, we won't ever move toward people different from us. Passionate people change their world and embrace the tension.

Passion helps us ignore the haters. Passion creates a laser focus. Passion is contagious and draws in the right people to help us. Petit would have never accomplished his dreams without passion, and we will never exist within the in-between if we are not passionate about doing so!

It Takes Persistence

The next big lesson for us from our story is the importance of persistence. Philippe and his team had every reason to doubt their success and quit, many times over. One team member did drop out in the eleventh hour. But the rest persisted. In the face of looming security guards, equipment struggles, a foot injury (he stepped on a nail), and an ever-shrinking timeline, the team persisted.

I think the reason most people don't live the life they dream of is a lack of persistence. Life is difficult. Things happen. Excuses are everywhere. The easy road is ever present. But those who persist experience a life most people only dream about. Embracing tension for the long run will never happen unless we persist.

You will get hurt if you try.

There I said it. Every great story, real or fiction, involves a struggle. We love great stories, but we hate the life required to tell one. Persistence says, "I will move forward." No struggle, no tension, no decision is too hard for the persistent person.

It Takes Preparation

This is probably the most important lesson you can learn in the face of the high-wire walk of table-building; if we aren't prepared we will stumble and fall. And when the stakes are high the fall is further than we can imagine. So, be prepared.

Philippe Petit did thousands of practice walks. He and his team simulated everything they could before their experience. They had models of the buildings and equipment. They studied each building dozens of times. They recruited help. They knew the physics, the psychology, and the architecture. They were prepared.

I feel at this point that many of us are imagining more education, more apologetics, more proof, better arguments for our beliefs. Maybe you're getting excited about preparing to destroy that person with whom you disagree.

If you're thinking this way, go back and read chapters one through three.

You've clearly missed the point. If your preparation leads you toward confidence in battle, you'll never survive the tension. One broken argument, one exposed wrong idea, one poorly worded point made—any of these will destroy your pride and you will fall. Even worse you'll hang on in belligerent defiance, making you irrelevant.

Preparation may include sharpening your beliefs, but more than anything it will be practicing humility and listening. Most people with strong ideas don't have a problem with spouting those tenets. They struggle to listen to someone else who disagrees. Without careful listening, the discourse is meaningless.

I know, because this is the most difficult thing for me. I talk to think. Others may think to talk. That's probably preferable. Either way, I know my tendencies to interject, interrupt, and insist on my way. So, my preparation requires lessons in listening. For you it may be the same, or you may need to understand your professed beliefs better. Maybe you need to study up on the other side.

No matter what your preparation needed, we all need to prepare for meaningful discourse, especially if we care about other people and their worth as human beings.

Most of us will never embrace the tension it takes to create space to discuss life and faith. But when we do, if we do, life will open up like never before. The rush of truly living and existing within the in-between will sweep over us and take us to new levels of consciousness. We will be included in conversations and opportunities like never before. We will gain influence we could have never imagined.

Step out. Be brave. Be prepared, persistent, and passionate. Live in the tension!

CHAPTER FIVE

Words Matter

What's Said at the Table

Whatever words we utter should be chosen with care
for people will hear them and be influenced by them for good or ill.
—Buddha

St. Jerome, the patron saint of translation, is one of the most unique saints in all of Catholicism. He reached sainthood differently than other saints. He was awarded this status through services rendered to the church rather than through some sort of miracle or sanctification achievement. He was very important in translating the Bible from Hebrew to Latin, in an early time of the new language.

But he is famous for more than just important translation. St. Jerome is known for a pretty interesting translation mistake. One that led to art, by people like Michelangelo, representing key biblical figures with less than accurate traits—like Moses with horns!

In his Latin version of the Old Testament, St. Jerome inadvertently altered a well-known biblical moment. When Moses descended the mountain with the Ten Commandments, we are told that his face was "radiant." Due to some Hebrew language nuances, he accidentally translated the word for "radiant" as "horns." He gave Moses horns. People read this, believed this, and even began to imagine the Old Testament prophet with horns.

The Importance of Words

This is a silly illustration of a very real issue in our current, globalized culture of communication. Even within the over seven thousand languages in the world, there are differences in dialect, grammar, and vocabulary. Language is dynamic and therefore constantly moving, changing, and evolving. No one language is more complex or powerful than another. To the native speaker, each language offers critical substance to their thoughts, feelings, actions, and plans.

Words are how we express ourselves. Often the subjectivity of phrasing and meaning isn't conveyed as we might hope. This can lead to major misunderstandings. I once heard a professor say that a large percentage of conflict is a result of miscommunication, and most conflict resolution boils down to understanding exactly what each other is trying to say.

This is why counseling is so important in marriage. Men and women are different. Husbands and wives say things differently and understand meaning differently based on their personal history. Counseling provides a safe space and a mediator to help clarify communication.

Too often we assume meaning behind words. Have you ever received a text to which you applied tone? Have you ever sent an email with one intention, yet it was read with an implied meaning behind the words you used and everything blew up? Yeah. We all have. Words are important. They are one universal way that humans exchange ideas. But there's not a universal language, syntax, or dialect, and that makes things difficult.

The dynamic characteristics of language are probably the most frustrating factors when trying to have meaningful discussion around important

matters. Political correctness has paralyzed so many of us and keeps people from engaging in conversation with someone of a different worldview,
race, gender, or religion. In an ever-growing, easily offended society, it
may seem impossible to ask questions and truly understand each other.

Worrying about being labeled differently than you see yourself is a
real fear, keeping many people from expressing themselves. So, people
hide behind social media platforms. They shout their beliefs digitally.
They ignore, hide, and unfriend those who might disagree or argue.
Words have never been more important than now, because people
are reading text alone, without tone, body language, or facial expression, and trying to interpret meaning.

Important matters are being expressed more often by more people,
but the world has actually gotten quieter. People are less interactive.
People are less engaged. And people are more divided.

Words matter. Their importance is undisputed. And they are a large
part of what we use to describe the way we view the world. Discourse
is tricky because words are limited, inexact, and diversely defined. So,
what do we do about our words?

Let's look at some helpful ideas on using our words most effectively
when discussing important matters. Especially when those across the
table fundamentally disagree.

Using Words Well

I want to try to help us all have better discussions. Discussions that help
people are healthy for individuals, groups, and society. Understanding
a few key components of discourse and how we can enhance them
will make us more skilled at using our words. Words matter, so let's
use them well.

Simplicity Trumps Complexity

This is a great rule to understand when teaching, discussing, or coaching. All of these activities use words, and our temptation is to move toward complexity. Come on...you know it makes you feel good when you can confuse someone with your expert knowledge and articulation of a subject. But people are more inclined to learn, grow, and converse when they truly understand.

It's not helpful or healthy to use a ten-dollar word when a two-dollar word will do. We'll discuss this again later in another chapter, but the simple idea is the idea of simplicity. When a person can explain complex ideas simply, they tend to grow an audience. More people want to listen in and exchange ideas. Complexity makes us feel better. But simplicity reaches the masses.

Simplicity trumps complexity when helping people understand what matters most!

Define As You Go

Inevitably, when discussing matters of importance, we will come across jargon. This is almost unavoidable. The key is to define as you go. This relates to simplicity. It shows you are humble enough to understand that you understand a language that the other might not. You know exactly what I mean. In my world, we call it "Christianese." But it doesn't just exist in church world. Every field of study, area of business, and religion (including atheism) has its own language used to explain certain nuances within that world.

There's nothing wrong with that. Simply define. Be willing to humbly explain what you mean. Most people will appreciate your honesty. Face it, people will pretend to understand to save face. You may think you're having the same discussion and you're on the same page when, in fact, you've alienated the listener. Are you self-aware enough to admit you've done this? That's okay. Next time, define.

Listen Better, Speak Better

Maybe you're a gifted speaker. Maybe not. Either way, you'll be better at speaking if you can get better at listening. I'm the kind of person that tends to think about what I'm going to say next when the other person is speaking. Instead, I should be listening intently and humbly considering what they have to say. That human across the table is important. Their opinion matters, not because it's right, but because it's theirs.

One of the major benefits of actually listening to the other is having a real conversation. If you only share your thoughts, think of something new, and then share that, you're not actually discussing anything. You're basically talking to yourself with someone else there. Listening is a crucial part of discussing. And one very important thing begins to happen when we begin to listen...relationship! We begin to care about this other person. We don't see an issue anymore, we see a person—flesh and blood, emotions, personal history. We peek into another life and begin to understand.

At this point, our words get better because they know how to reach the heart of this person we are understanding and loving.

Think To Talk

Some people think to talk while others talk to think. I'm a part of the latter. This makes conversation difficult. I feel like I end up saying too much and listening too little. I'm working hard to listen well and think before I speak. When we consider what we are saying, our words are used more skillfully. Too often people say things they mean in a mean way, because they haven't thought about their words.

Considering what we are saying and how we are saying it is crucial to healthy, helpful conversation. This is especially true when discussing things that really matter. These discussions tend to make us passionate, and passion tends to speak from the heart and not the mind. We all know people who speak with passion at the expense of consideration. We've all heard an impassioned speech that comes across hatefully, but spoken better could have expressed love.

We are better when we consider others in our words. Think to talk. Then you can communicate effectively and compassionately!

Words matter. They are a huge part of how we express our thoughts, feeling, plans, actions, and beliefs. They are inexact. They are tricky. But we can gain skill in using them effectively. Let's work on our words!

CHAPTER SIX

Disagreeing Agreeably

Some Ideas About Discussion

If I am walking with two other men, each of them will serve as my teacher.
I will pick out the good points of the one and imitate them,
and the bad points of the other and correct them in myself.

—Confucius

In the world of Facebook and Twitter, Fox News and CNN, viral videos and instant news feeds, the world is more publicly divided than ever. Things we would once only know about a person close to us, we now know about strangers. Their views, beliefs, politics, and frustrations are plastered all over a "wall" we can all see. We are more connected than ever, yet we are further from each other than we even realize.

So many strong opinions and views voiced to the world means the world needs to learn how to discuss and disagree at the same time. The catchphrase "have a conversation" or "let's start a discussion" is used so often by people who really just want a voice and a seat at the table. There's nothing wrong with that. I believe we should all get a seat at the table. But we must not mask the desire for power and recognition behind a cry for equality.

People disagree.

There, I said it. And that's okay. We all see the world through lenses we've developed over time, experiences, and education. There's no one you'll always agree with all of the time. My wife and I love each other deeply. We spend a lot of time together. Our core values are the same. And we still disagree often. That's okay. Disagreement challenges us to learn, grow, expand perception, and empathize with that person who exists on the other side of us.

The key is learning to have meaningful conversation while disagreeing. I believe it's possible. But we have to be serious about learning how to do it. Passions surface when discussing important matters. This can cause us to be emotional. In itself, passionate, emotional conversation isn't wrong. But I'll be the first to admit, when I get too passionate in a disagreement, I'm more likely to say something I'll regret. Also, when discussing differences, we may feel the other side isn't learning, processing, or taking seriously our views. At this moment, it's wise to settle our own hearts and strive to discuss with only one agenda… love!

I want to explore a few ideas that relate to having better conversations with "the other." The first are some dangerous assumptions we often make when trying to discuss our beliefs. These few things can destroy a potentially helpful dialogue. Then we will look into how we can organize a discussion to perpetuate more healthy, helpful conversation with those with whom we disagree.

4 Dangerous Assumptions When Discussing While Disagreeing

1.) This person is like me.

Let me help with this one by saying right away, they aren't like you! Whew, now we can move on to more important things. I believe that spiritual diversity is even greater than physical, and they are both beautiful. Notice I didn't say everyone was right. I didn't say truth doesn't matter. I just said that diversity is beautiful.

I know what I believe and I really believe it. I'm okay with the fact that someone doesn't. Do I want to see that person find truth? Sure. And even in that I'm assuming the basis of what I believe is absolute truth. I look at it like this; if someone is searching out spiritual matters, they are closer to knowing the true God than someone who isn't. Either way, just because someone isn't like you doesn't mean you cannot have an amazing conversation about faith.

2.) This person knows what I know.

Entering a spiritual conversation with this assumption leads people to use jargon. Every faith, mystic, and religion has an insider language. Assuming that everyone knows that language can hurt our dialogue. We end up talking in circles, often about the same things.

Also, jargon causes one person to feel superior and the other, inferior. This is never helpful. No one wants to converse with arrogance. We lose influence and credibility when we begin to explain deeply spiritual matters in a language foreign to our listener. It requires our conscious effort to speak to people in a common vernacular and avoid your preferred jargon.

3.) This person is completely wrong.

For starters, this disposition is the opposite of humility, and pride limits effectiveness. Also, all truth is God's truth. If you believe that God (or whatever your word for God) is the author of truth, then even if people are wrong about some things, in your opinion or faith, they might be correct in other things.

Common ground is the best place to begin spiritual discussions. Find that ground and engage from there. It may be a story from the past. It may be the idea that both parties believe something similar about God or faith. From there a meaningful conversation can happen because we begin to connect rather than deflect.

4.) This person will never change.

Most people change. You are changing right now. You're getting older. You're learning new things. You're awakening to new ideas all the time. You're moving through seasons of life. You're becoming more or less of what you hope to be. People change.

Sometimes it's slow. Sometimes we don't even realize it. But people change. Our influence reaches further and deeper than we can imagine. To assume that people you're connecting with spiritually aren't going to change short-changes the meaning behind having these conversations in the first place. Give people your time. Give them your energy. Give them your presence. Then give them space to grow.

Far too often people are anxious to sit and discuss tension points with people with whom they disagree. There's too great a sense of instability found in their belief or in the knowledge of their belief to engage someone who might be more polished or articulate about these matters.

Also, there could be animosity or sense of "war raging" against those who don't have a similar worldview. Sometimes that war is raged against those who maybe even agree similarly on an issue, but ultimately find the solution to be found in different places.

Basically, people want to...

be right.

make a point.

convert thinking.

You might be reading this now and feel something deep within; insecurity, truth, anger, confusion.

These kinds of discussions are my passion. I like embracing the awkwardness. I've given my life to engaging in faith discussions with people from all walks of life in the downtown district of Las Vegas. I want these discussions to be meaningful for myself and others.

My hope is that people...

feel free to disagree and still be friends.

begin to seek truth and not just hold a "party line."

love each other because of differences, not in spite of them.

With this hope in mind I've discovered and formulated...

4 Keys to Discussing While Disagreeing:

1.) Start a Conversation

One of the rules I use for my blog and podcast where I discuss faith is "it's about conversations, not conversions." I feel like this bothers people at their core because most people who believe strongly about anything that shapes their life tend to promote their brand of life change and convert others to their way of thinking.

Ever met a die-hard vegan? They have an agenda. Do you have a fitness guru friend? They have a plan for you. This isn't a bad thing. It's proof of passion. But it's also a turnoff.

Just like that friend who's trying to get you involved in their "multilevel marketing" opportunity (pyramid scheme), you tend to avoid anyone who seems to only care about selling you a new way to change your life. Yeah, I'm talking about you, Plexus rep. It's not a lack of passion that causes me to focus on conversations rather than conversions. It's the exact opposite. I want to build bridges to people because I'm passionate about people.

The only people Jesus quickly shut down with seemingly abrasive truth were the religious elite who had oppressed the very people he had come to save. Everyone else got conversation over dinner, at a party, or at natural meeting places in town.

If you want to successfully discuss faith with someone different from you, start a conversation.

2.) Set a Goal

It's okay to go into an awkward discussion with goals in mind, as long as that goal isn't "winning" an argument. Honest discussions about a topic as intimate as faith, race, passion, and education will not happen if anyone present feels attacked.

Approach people with goals like...

> *building a genuine relationship.*
>
> *developing deeper personal, emotional, relational, or spiritual connection.*

learning something about a person, faith, idea, or worldview previously foreign.

creating influence and speak-ability in a new area or culture.

These kinds of goals create open dialogue that can truly move disagreements forward. A personal goal will help you stay on track and remain humble throughout the interaction. You may even want to go a step further if the interaction has explosive potential and set predetermined goals with the other person.

In her 2010 TEDWomen talk, Elizabeth Lesser explained her Take "the Other" to Lunch initiative and how she uses goal setting to help her connect with women who disagree with her politically. She tells of one lunch conversation in which the women agreed on a set of guidelines to help them reach a common goal of civil conversation. Great idea!

Goal setting helps maintain civility and humility when disagreeing over dynamic issues.

3.) Seek to Understand

One great leadership lesson that I learned recently is best spoken by St. Francis of Assisi...

"Seek first to understand, then to be understood."

This idea is reinforced by Stephen Covey in his book, *7 Habits of Highly Effective People*. It's difficult to understand another person if all you're doing during a conversation is...

thinking of what you're going to say next.

dismissing everything they are saying.

considering yourself smarter, better, more experienced, or greater.

Also, it's increasingly difficult to truly understand someone's perspective and beliefs when you don't care. Compassion for others draws us into their story and creates understanding.

Now, don't confuse understanding with agreement. I can understand why a person hates God or organized religion without agreeing that they should or agreeing that I do. That's a huge misconception. We think that listening and understanding means agreeing or condoning.

We don't have to change our position, but we may need to change our posture if we are truly going to seek to understand.

4.) Simplify Your Terminology

Because we tend to approach a disagreement with the goal of winning the argument, we begin to load our arsenal with weapons of terminology. We believe if we can get someone back on their heels because they don't understand our words, wording, or word usage, then we can come out on top of the conversation.

When people feel attacked by your "intellect" and borrowed five-dollar words, they get emotional. At this point you've lost them and you've lost influence.

The other extreme can be true as well. While we don't want to over-intellectualize the conversation, we also don't want to treat people like they're stupid. Talking down to someone by sarcastically dumbing down the explanation of your beliefs is demeaning and the lowest form of true debate.

Talk to people like you would want to be talked to, and you're sure to create brilliantly effective dialogue.

Maybe you're a Christian who needs to take your atheist coworker to lunch next week. Maybe you're a politically liberal Democrat who needs to truly listen to your staunchly Republican brother-in-law. Maybe you're just one human being who isn't listening enough to anyone who thinks, believes, and behaves differently from you.

Try some of these ideas and work on your conversations. You might even come to love someone you never imagined you could. You might learn something you never imagined you would. And you might even move in a direction you never imagined you should.

Discussing while disagreeing is possible. It's even healthy. But it doesn't happen best in social media posts or news media blasts. It happens in community, face-to-face, around a table. It happens in common areas, person to person.

True compassion is extended to those with whom we agree and disagree. Anyone can love a friend. Stand out by loving an enemy and inviting them to the table!

PART THREE

Put Legs On It

No matter what message you are about to deliver somewhere, whether it is holding out a hand of friendship, or making clear that you disapprove of something, is the fact that the person sitting across the table is a human being, so the goal is to always establish common ground.

—Madeleine Albright

Now that we've worked to create an amazing, engaging tabletop, it's time to put legs on it. The legs of a table are the unsung heroes. You really only notice them if you stub a toe or slam a knee. But they are holding up the table. They make the table what it is. The legs of the table may be unseen but they are not unimportant.

For us, the legs of the table are the parts of us that need to be embraced and transformed. They are the foundational aspects of following Jesus in faith. They also make creating space for discussion possible. The better our legs, the better our table. The better our table, the more chairs and people and energy.

I want to say a few things about this section and the legs of our table before moving on. First, everything in you is going to fight against the development of these four legs. You'll want to make excuses. You'll try and use the Bible to push back. You might even say, "But that's not how it's done" a few times. Stop. Create. Open up. And let's think through this together.

Second, this final section is the practical aspect to this book. It's the point. It's about what happens in you so you can create space to discuss life and faith. So, if it catches in your heart, you may begin to shift perspective. If you start acting like you believe these things, your world will get bigger, and those with small perspectives will frustrate you.

Don't get angry. Remember, you were there too. The key is to love these people as well. The ones who just don't get it need you to help them build bigger tables. The tendency is to redirect our pride rather than getting rid of it altogether. We must avoid this if we truly want a bigger table.

Lastly, you may begin to view your church as incomplete in its expression of love to others. Jesus models radical, inclusive love and grace. But that doesn't mean his church always does. As your table gets bigger, you'll begin to notice how small your church's table may be. Again, love well. But also, be aware that a new community of faith may be necessary for next steps.

CHAPTER SEVEN

Our First Leg: Humility

Making Room at the Table

You can believe something with so much conviction that you'd die for that belief, and yet in the exact same moment you can also say, "I could be wrong..." This is because conviction and humility, like faith and doubt, are not opposites; they're dance partners.

—Rob Bell, *What We Talk About When We Talk About God*

We're building a table. A bigger table. A table with room for everyone to experience the grace of God. Making room at the table begins with humility; there's not enough room for you, your pride, and them. Pride pushes the "other" away from the table, if they even make it that far to begin with.

So, we have to deal with it. We must address our ever-present struggle with our ever- present ego-self. I'm not coming from a place of victory over this struggle. I'm in the struggle. Every day I see my need to kill my ego and resurrect Christ-likeness.

If anything, Jesus was humble.

Sit with that for a second. Really. Meditate on that truth.

Are you now ready to learn humility from Jesus? Let's discover the transformational path that leads to humble presence.

Contracting Self

Tzimtzum

The Hebrew mystics use this term to describe how they interpret God at creation. Viewing God as infinite, they understand all of the universe as filled with his presence. Therefore, for anything else to exist, God must have contracted or withdrawn to allow room for us and creation. While this term is not found in the Bible, it is still an interesting idea worth exploring. I believe we see this in Jesus, and the author of John's gospel tells us...

> No one has ever seen God. But the unique One, who is himself near to the Father's heart. He has revealed God to us.

Let's look into the life and words of Jesus and see what we can learn about humility. About contracting our presence so others can fit at the table. Dying to our false selves and living out of our true selves as originally designed by God.

Pouring Out Ourselves

We've already discussed the ingredients for continuity within the church, which includes humility. But let's dive deeper into the letter of Paul to the church at Philippi. Paul gives this description of Jesus becoming human while remaining Divine…

> Though he was God, he did not think of equality with God as something to cling to.
>
> Instead, he gave up his divine privileges…

In the original language, Greek, we find that this term for giving up his divine privileges literally means he "emptied himself." Jesus poured out his self, his identity as God, and his power to become human and experience life as we do. For Jesus to live out his purpose on earth, he had to stoop down in the ultimate act of humility.

Coming to earth as a King of kings would have been a step down for Jesus. But he took it a step further. Paul continues to describe the extent of Jesus' humility.

> …he took the humble position of a slave [or the form of a slave] and was born as a human being.

Jesus took on human form…step down one. And then took on the lowest of human positions and forms a slave…step two. To reach the oppressed, Jesus became oppressed. To reach the outcast, Jesus became an outcast.

Think with me a little further. The Jesus story includes that he was born of a virgin. We look at that in faith and celebrate. But imagine being a member of his community at that time. Mary shows up pregnant with no husband. Joseph's fiancée is pregnant and he swears it isn't his. They say it's a child of the Divine. Sure.

Jesus would've been largely, if not completely, viewed as a bastard child. Even within his small community he would've been ostracized and viewed as "unclean." Maybe that's why he was so comfortable with tax collectors and sinners. He understood what it felt like to be hated and ostracized. And why did he understand? Because he humbled himself. Not just in mind but in experience.

Let's keep going.

Remember that last supper Jesus had with his disciples before he was arrested and killed? Sure you do. You've seen the painting. As Jesus invites his disciples (not just "the Twelve" but others as well) to sit at the table, he does something mind-blowing. He washes their feet.

Their feet weren't like ours. It's bad enough to wash feet after they've been in socks and shoes all day. It's quite another to wash feet after they've walked in sandals down dirt roads behind animals all day. He didn't have gloves. He had water and a towel. He hiked up his robe, knelt down, and took the position of the lowest house servant by washing the feet of his followers.

The most powerful, important, influential person in the room used his power and influence for the benefit of others. Why? One reason I can think of was to show them what real love, acceptance, grace, and inclusion look like. They look like humility. He was about to welcome them into the Kingdom, to sit at the table with the King. He couldn't make room for them if he was the only one filling the room.

Jesus had to contract himself for the sake of others.

This kind of loving humility would change the game. He follows this action with a new command for them. This new command:

> So now I am giving you a new commandment: Love each other. Just as I have loved you, you should love each other. Your

love for one another will prove to the world that you are my disciples.

The Ten Commandments were good but outdated. Jesus had a new, all-encompassing command that would sum them up and simplify the very life of a disciple. Love. Not regular love. Not love as they had ever understood it before. Love like Jesus had loved them. The kind of love demonstrated by the most important person in the room serving others in the lowest form imaginable.

That's a new way of loving.

This kind of contracting, withdrawing, is an example for us. It's not theory or theology. It's practical. Let me take a stab at some very real ways you might need to withdraw yourself so someone else can make it to the table.

Poured Out Politics

Did I just say that? Yep!

What if we were so humble the only political view we shared was one of love? This may take the form of not posting that meme, not open-ly celebrating politicians as the saviors of America. Maybe you don't make that comment. You bite your tongue at the holiday gathering.

I'm not saying you sacrifice your political views. That might happen eventually. I'm talking about sacrificing the voicing, pushing, and pro-moting of those views, taking a gentler stance, a humbler position, a position of a servant or slave who would have disagreed politically with their master but would never have been allowed to communicate that disagreement.

That's radically humble.

Poured Out Theology

Work with me here. Again, I'm not saying you don't develop a meaningful theology that leads you to understand God in new and exciting ways. I am saying that we handle our theology with care.

Rather than being quick to toss out the heretic card, we toss the humility card. We wash the feet of those with whom we disagree. True spiritual transformation will not happen until we can humbly learn from the "other."

Let me illustrate this with a story.

I grew up Baptist, in an especially critical, segregated form of Baptist. Catholics were the enemy. They were the "Great Whore" from the Book of Revelation. You couldn't associate with a Catholic. And you certainly couldn't learn from a Catholic priest, bishop, Jesuit, Franciscan, etc.

But there I was. Sitting in a room with various denominations and theological streams represented. We were at a counseling center here in Vegas. I was there for the free food and to accompany a friend who was pursuing a counseling degree. The special speaker that day was William A. Barry, SJ, a Jesuit priest with all sorts of degrees and experience helping people follow Jesus into deep spiritual, mental, and relational healing.

He was a white-haired, elderly gentleman. Standing was a task for his aging body, so he occasionally leaned on the stool beside him. He spoke softly. He explained the suffering of God. I had never heard anything like this. God suffers because things aren't the way God desires. People suffer and the Comforter suffers alongside. This was new, refreshing, and thought-provoking. I was in awe.

Then it happened. Someone from a drastically different theological background decided to correct everyone's theology. They had an answer for this. God wasn't suffering. And he wanted to let everyone know. So, he raised his hand and boldly explained the "truth" about God getting what God wants. It sounded good. It sounded theological. It sounded intellectual. It didn't sound humble, loving, open, or gracious.

There was a palpable tension. The room got uncomfortable. This incredibly experienced, godly, humble man was challenged. His view of God was being "corrected" publicly. He was the guest speaker. How dare this man call him down like this. Was an argument about to happen? Would he concede? I waited with bated breath to see what would happen next.

Then, like only an eighty-year-old man of God could do, this Catholic Jesuit responded...

"Well, it seems that you know God better than I do."

Let me explain. If I had said this you would experience sarcasm at its best. But that wasn't his tone. He was truly humble. He sincerely lowered himself in front of everyone. The most intelligent person in the room, the keynote speaker, demonstrated a Christ-like humility I had never before seen. No male leader from my background would've done that. If challenged, you fight back. Stand up. Get loud.

Leadership was not humility. It was bravado. But not in this case. And not with Jesus. This man knelt down and washed his objector's feet in front of us all. He left no question in anyone's mind about his relationship to God, Jesus, and others. It was loving humility!

These are just a couple of examples where we could all practice humility like Jesus. We see in him a way forward. A way to love and include, less of me, more of them, a bigger table.

Let's continue crafting this leg of humility. It's not about passive contractions away from the table. There's an active element to humility, and it's summed up in one word.

Listening

Learning Empathy

No one explains and expresses empathy quite like Brené Brown. In her book *Daring Greatly*, Brown encourages us to live courageously by entering life with vulnerability and empathy. The shame we experience can be pushed back by opening up and sharing, as well as listening to others as they open up to us.

Here's a few ways she explains empathy:

Empathy conveys a simple acknowledgment. "You're not alone."

Empathy is connection; it's a ladder out of the shame hole.

Empathy doesn't require that we have the exact same experiences as the person sharing their story with us.

Empathy is connecting with the emotion that someone is experiencing, not the event or the circumstance.

Empathy is impossible without non-judgmental listening. And listening is impossible without humility. Can someone we know little about and have little in common with believe they can come to our home, our church, or our table and be heard? Probably not. There's no space for it.

Humility creates space; space to listen, space to hear, space for meaningful presence, not solving problems.

Listening is the catalyst for relationships. As human beings, we naturally gravitate to those we feel we can relate to, and people become more relatable when they feel free to share. If there's a table and chairs, people can share with other people. Tables. Chairs. People. Energy. Now add relationship. At this point, everything begins to change. We see people as people, and not ideas and philosophies and worldviews and politics and theologies we hate.

Listening to people is better than listening to ideas. People matter. We can love people without loving their ideas.

The key to getting people to share their stories is asking questions and not making statements. Conversations begin with genuine interest in the other person. Jesus was really great at this. When asked questions he felt were coming from an authentic heart, he would answer with another question. "How do you see it?"

This would get the other person sharing. Asking good questions is an art form. Questions come from curiosity. It's difficult to be curious about another when we are only interested in ourselves. Humility, contracting, making space, listening. These aspects of the table must be present if the table is to stand the test of time and be big enough to include every nation, every language, and every tribe.

This leg is directly connected to our next, very important leg of the table, *uncertainty*.

The first step in creating space to discuss life and faith is humbly acknowledging that all of life is faith and you could be wrong!

CHAPTER EIGHT

The Second Leg: Uncertainty

We Could Be Wrong...That's Faith

An intellectual is going to have doubts, for example, about a fundamentalist
religious doctrine that admits no doubt, about an imposed political system
that allows no doubt, about a perfect aesthetic that has no room for doubt.

—Antonio Tabucchi

It's Everywhere We Look

A big step in creating space for meaningful discourse about things that
matter most is realizing how much we humans operate in faith. Many
intellectuals will argue that they only operate from a point of evidence
and proof. But that isn't a complete view of the human experience.

The quicker we acknowledge an everywhere, everyday faith as crucial
to being human, the quicker we will be willing and able to discuss life
with people with whom we disagree.

Faith isn't just about religion. Sure, it's a huge part of any ancient tradition. But it's not exclusively religious. From the person who believes
in nothing to the person who believes in everything, faith is present
and accounted for. It's healthy to understand this about ourselves and
the world around us.

And it's important to acknowledge…"I could be wrong."

"But, Dad, what if we're wrong"

Father and son ride silently to the park for the Saturday morning Little League game. It's a big game for the son, and like most fathers, Dad is feeling the pressure more than his boy. The air is thick with the sound of cool air blowing, talk radio chatting, and nervous cleats tapping the inside of the passenger-side door. Dad thinks he knows what's going on in his boy's mind, and before too much longer his son just blurts it out…

"What if we're wrong? I mean…there are so many people who believe so many things. What if we're wrong? What if Jesus wasn't real? What if it's someone else? What if someone else is right and we're wrong about what we believe!"

The dad just sits there, shocked. He can't believe that this is on the mind of his ten-year-old on the morning of such a big game. Apparently, it's been on his mind. What does he say? How do you respond to that? What are they teaching in Sunday School?

The thoughts quickly come and go, all the while the son stares, penetrating his father with questioning eyes. Dad recognizes this eventually and struggles to get out an answer. After stumbling over ideas and words, he finally says…

"It's faith! That's really what faith is. We don't know for sure, but we trust that what we believe is the truth. I guess we could be wrong. But we trust. We trust that Jesus was who he said he was. We don't know for sure, exactly. We just trust. That's faith!"

Maybe you're a dad who takes his family to church regularly and you've had this conversation. Maybe you've had the same questions but never felt the freedom to ask them. Maybe you're confused about people who are so sure about what they believe. Maybe you're feeling like I'm saying "maybe" a lot?

Either way, we all understand this conversation about religion. But what if your child asked you the same thing about the science of origin? What if you don't adhere to a religious system and your child comes home from school and asks...

"Mom, how did something come from nothing for no reason? Why would nothing do that? What if my science teacher is wrong? What if we didn't come from nothing and there's more out there? What is there if we're wrong?"

I know I wouldn't have answers. I'm willing to bet that unless you're a physicist you would struggle articulating a response. And face it...no physicists are reading this book. Ultimately, your answer would boil down to faith and belief in science that you may not fully understand handed to you by people you've never met.

I mean, at some point the smartest people in the world believed the earth was flat.

And don't get me started on Pluto's planetary status and the health factors in eggs. Remember when they were good for you, then bad, then the white part was good and the yellow bad, then it turns out the yellow part is packed with the really good stuff.

We can forgive someone for not placing unadulterated trust in an ever-expanding, maturing system in search of knowledge.

So, let's look at faith a little further and see if we can put some common understanding around the word, the idea, and the practice as it relates to our everyday human experience.

"Believe me, it's not about proof"

A formal, yet summed-up definition of faith: strong belief or trust in someone or something for which there is no proof.

According to the letter to the Hebrews in the New Testament, we see faith defined as the confidence that what we actually hope for will happen; it gives us assurance about things we cannot see.

Let's examine these ideas a bit and see if we can find a common understanding and language for what we mean when we say faith.

First, there are a couple of key words right away that need addressing: belief and trust or confidence and hope. Belief is basically a state of mind based on a feeling of confidence in someone or something.

We believe things every day. We believe the sun will come up in the morning. We are confident in our ability to continue breathing, thinking, and operating as we did yesterday. Trust is attached to belief. Think of trust as the legs of belief. If belief is a mental state based on feelings, intellect, and emotion, trust becomes the body that acts out those feelings and thoughts.

Belief is soul. Trust is body.

They are attached and inextricably linked.

Hope is connected, too, in a powerful way. It's the expectant side of our little faith "person" we are constructing. Hope is a relatable human condition. It's the fuel behind so much of the actions we take every day.

We hope tomorrow will be better. We hope our children will be smarter, more talented, and better resourced than ourselves. We hope in a preferred future.

Hope pushes people to amazing things. The state of constant anticipation that something will happen or is true propels people to greatness. Every underdog story contains hope. It's intangible, yet powerful. It's the energy that moves our faith "person" forward through every circumstance.

Are you feeling more and more like a person of faith? Are you seeing that faith isn't about what's provable? Are you shifting to the center of this discussion? I hope so!

Next, in our definition of faith we come across an object, someone or something. Faith always has...

an object of focus.

a system, group, or ideal to hold on to.

a person, people, or a book to follow.

Again, this isn't just religious. Science could be the focus of the system. Science has its people and books. I know, I know...but science is proof. Even the theories? Science is full of flawed thinking, incomplete ideas, and yes, theories. A theory is simply a "belief" or idea proposed to be possibly true.

I want to be sure and explain, I'm not a scientist. But a basic understanding of the scientific method leads us to these understandings about the "belief" surrounding scientific discovery.

Scientists learn all the time how they were wrong at some point in history. They discover more and more all the time. New discoveries are the point of giving your life in search of knowledge. But...

...when someone says that we don't understand something fully right now, but we will, given enough time, that is, of course, a belief. That's faith. We aren't, at that point, talking about people of faith versus people of science; we're talking about people of faith, just faith in different things.

Not only is all of life belief, confidence, trust, and hope in an object, some-one, or something, but the reality is that there is always something we don't and/or won't know. This is humbling. This makes me feel small. In relation to all there is to know, what I know doesn't even make a dent.

If asked, "Do you have all knowledge?" any logical, right-minded person will say, "No."

I'm assuming every reader is a logical, right-minded person. I'm assuming my audience doesn't have "all knowledge." So, let's take this logic one question further. "Could it be possible that God, Spirit, the Divine exists in the other half of things you don't know?"

Again, a simple question based in simple logic with an understood answer of "Yes."

There's always the possibility because we are limited. Science and religion are not opposed. They aren't so different. They are simply operating from different objects of faith.

In this case, the argument isn't proof. The argument is object. We're all operating from faith. What's the object of your faith?

"It's faith in myself"

I showed up to the restaurant to meet Dylan. He's a huge influencer and connector in my community. He had agreed to be interviewed for my podcast. It's all about life and faith in downtown Las Vegas. This was a big deal to me. Getting this guy to talk about faith could get so many others to engage in similar conversations.

As I sat down, we exchanged greetings and I was caught off guard by the number of people he was eating with. Sitting at the table was Dylan's new friend, an unexpected, up-and-coming atheist spokesperson.

"Jeremy thinks it requires as much faith to be an atheist as it does to be a Christian."

This phrase was directed to his friend, and I was totally flustered on the inside. I think I kept calm on the outside. Never let 'em see you sweat, right?

His friend stared off thoughtfully, examining the statement. I couldn't help but think I had been set up. Sabotaged. I was sure I had been lured there to argue for my faith. Fortunately, that wasn't the case.

"I guess that's true. It's just faith in myself, not some other thing."

Whew! A response that didn't provoke an argument. In fact, this response took down any and all walls to further discourse on the matter. We began openly talking about the faith of an atheist and the faith of a Christian. I don't think any of us imagined such healthy conversation, but it happened.

Fast-forward a few months, and again I found myself in cordial conversation about faith with a professed atheist. He even claimed he was atheist before it was cool to not believe in God. I decided to throw out Dylan's move. I equated the faith of Christianity and atheism.

Again, he agreed.

"I'm just trusting in myself."

I was starting to see a common thread. Intelligent, rational humans who don't believe in God were willing to acknowledge that their views were still belief based on a hope in something they couldn't prove.

Discussions about life and faith happen best when space is created to acknowledge common ground and common language.

Maybe you're convinced by now. Maybe not. But I want to continue to explore the idea of faith and what it really is and how we should all have the guts to admit…

"I could be wrong."

Necessary Uncertainty

I remember my wife's persistent, penetrating question as we talked of starting a church in Downtown Las Vegas…

"What if it doesn't work?"

I couldn't wrap my mind around that option. Something "not working" wasn't even in my realm of thinking. But she was right to ask the question. The truth of the matter is…

it could absolutely fall apart.

most startup churches eventually fail.

this was going to be our biggest leap of faith ever.

The flipside of the faith coin is doubt, darkness, and uncertainty

Without doubt, darkness, and uncertainty, it's not really faith. If every question is answered, if every plan is perfectly aligned and in place, if every step is taken only after everything has been made certain, it's not really faith.

"Faith without doubt leads to moral arrogance, the eternal pratfall of the religiously convinced."

—Joe Klein

The Christian faith is based on, well, just that—faith. From creation to Jesus, from the Jewish temple to the early church, it's all based on a faith in God. A faith that trusts God is everything revealed in the scriptures. A faith that trusts Jesus is the only way to new life and lasting transformation.

But it's also a faith that asks its followers to trust Jesus' word and way above all else. I tend to think that Christians don't exercise their faith in Jesus because they operate their lives out of fear rather than faith. They make decisions from the wrong side of the coin.

Uncertainty cannot hinder faith because they are attached at the hip. Embracing the unknown is a necessary aspect of faith. Explaining faith in every detail doesn't change the fact that there's always an uncertainty.

I recently heard the philosopher Terence McKenna remark that even science asks for one big miracle when it comes to evolution and the Big Bang theory. No matter how much "evidence" is drawn, the fact remains, it's a matter of faith because there's always a shadow of doubt. No one was there. It wasn't observed.

All of life is faith with uncertainty. You travel the streets hoping you don't get in an accident but knowing it's a possibility. You make choices every day hoping you are right but never really knowing what the future holds.

Live the tension. Love the tension.

The flipside of the coin of faith is uncertainty. On this I'm certain... wait...yeah, I'm certain!

It's okay…not knowing is the point

There is a big push in the Christian world to "explain" within reason the faith found in Jesus, the Bible, creationism, God, and more. The word for it is apologetics. For a time, I was fascinated with apologetics and reasonably arguing for my faith. There are some great people making great arguments.

And let's face it, I enjoy a good argument. I don't mean full-blown screaming and yelling, throwing things, and being hurtful with my words. I enjoy a logical, intellectual discussion around opposing views and/or opinions. It's fun to craft theories and arguments. I would have killed it in debate if I had that opportunity in high school.

I'll never forget hearing the story of Lee Strobel, an investigative journalist in Chicago. His wife became a Christian, but he was an atheist. There was real struggle for him around his wife's newfound faith. So, he set out on a mission.

With all of his investigative journalism resources, Mr. Strobel aimed to disprove Christianity and the claims of Jesus and the church. His goal was to prove there is no God and the Bible wasn't true.

Long story short, by the end of his investigation he was convinced. Not that God wasn't real, but rather that Jesus was exactly who he said he was, the Son of God. He has a series of fine books, *The Case for…*Faith, a Creator, Christ, etc. And he isn't the only story like this I've heard.

There are intellectuals from all walks of life throughout modern history who changed their views after a time of seeking out truth. This really works for some people. The issue exists when people want others to believe based purely on these intellectual findings. They shout REASON in hopes that reasonable people will believe what they believe.

Doesn't this diminish faith? If I can prove and reason my beliefs, is it even faith at all?

> "Nothing is more dangerous to one's own faith than the work of an apologist. No doctrine of that faith seems to me so spectral, so unreal as one that I have just successfully defended in a public debate."
>
> —C.S. Lewis

What about mystery? What about the beauty in not knowing? What about the spiritual? Apologetics may shift a person's thinking, but that doesn't necessarily mean it moves their heart. It's okay to not know! It's kind of the point. We don't "hope" in what is guaranteed. We hope in what we cannot see. And that's everyone, not just the religious.

When claiming faith as a fundamental human experience, I come across some strong opposition. As a matter of fact, people on Twitter have put me in all kinds of groups that paint me as, well, words I can't even say. To say the least they think I'm dumb.

One guy (or girl, it's hard to tell online) was especially hateful. This person took offense that I would claim they believe and behave in ways not based on absolute evidence and proof. He even told me as much. You would've thought I called him a rapist or pedophile. He was really offended.

But rationally we all move forward in life with some mystery, uncertainty, and doubt.

The chair you're sitting in right now as you read this is holding you up. You sat down trusting in the makers of that chair, in the materials they used, and in their engineering prowess to construct a chair to hold your weight. Trust me, I've placed my faith in a chair and its makers and been let down more than once.

THE SECOND LEG: UNCERTAINTY

Nothing says "I don't know and it's okay" like flying in an airplane. Sure, air travel is safer than automobile travel. Sure, there are statistics and science around flight that reassure us we will probably get to our destination safely. But planes crash. Things break. Explosions blow holes in the sides of planes and suck passengers out of the aircraft. Seriously, I read about that today in the news.

Science and religion can establish all of the evidence and proof they want, but we all know, the more we learn, the more we realize we don't know. Apologetics can be helpful, but it misses the point. Facts and figures don't explain the spiritual.

It's okay to not know…it's kind of the point!

There's a battle inside between uncertainty and pride

I think the biggest reason we struggle with the uncertainty of faith involves pride. Let me explain. Whether you are a leader in your field, in your religion, or in a nation, it works in your favor if you can be sure about the direction you are taking, and you can communicate certainty to those following your leadership.

No one follows the guy who stands up and says, "I've researched the best path for the future of this organization, and I sure hope the facts and figures I researched are real and true because we are going this direction either way, even though I'm not 100 percent sure I'm right."

That guy scares people. He doesn't get elected, hired, a following. Pastors can't really stand in front of a church and express transparent doubt. Professors can't lecture a class admitting they don't fully understand ideas and explain the holes in theories. People want leaders to lead and teachers to teach with certainty.

And certainty is contagious. We become certain the more someone else is certain. It doesn't matter that they are posturing in a way that masks their doubt. We love that. We gravitate to that. It's how people get followers.

I think there is something equally powerful in humility. When someone moves in a direction with humble confidence, it's attractive. Maybe not to weak-minded people who need someone else's strength to make it, but to strong-minded thinkers, a humbly confident leader is someone worth following.

That kind of leader can say, "I don't have all of the answers, but I'm going to believe _____ will happen. There's mystery, fear, and excitement ahead, but together we can wade through the unknown and follow the path that unfolds before us as we pursue a full life." Sure, there's not a lot of bravado in this phrase, but there's a ton of adventure and purpose.

Pride says, "I'm right and I don't care what you have to say."

Humility says, "I welcome all stories, ideas, and knowledge to the table."

Humble confidence goes a step further and says, "I'll hear you, respect you, grow closer to you, all while exercising my faith in a loving way because I could be wrong."

Hold On Loosely...But Don't Let Go

If I'm at a restaurant and there's a jukebox and it has the song "Hold On Loosely" by .38 Special, I will play that song and sing that song and be annoying. By the way, the same goes for "Hungry Like A Wolf." I don't know why, but I love playing those tunes on a jukebox.

Those words are a powerful reminder of what I call The Gripping Principle. The Gripping Principle goes like this; the tighter you hold on to something you feel slipping away, the greater loss of control you experience.

Every parent who has tried to use more rules and tighter restrictions on a rebellious teenager understands this principle. Anyone who's ever tried to hold water tightly in the palm of their hand has felt this principle. Greater control isn't found in stronger holds, and this scares people.

I'm learning it's possible to hold to belief and embrace uncertainty at the same time. I'm learning the secret to faith isn't assurance, but dependence—dependence on God, grace, hope, love, people, and Jesus. If you're seeking firm answers, you're probably not living the faith adventure.

CHAPTER NINE

Leg Number Three: Invitation

Welcoming Others to the Table

A real conversation always contains an invitation.
You are inviting another person to reveal herself or himself to you,
to tell you who they are or what they want.

—David Whyte

Making You Believe versus Inviting You to Believe

A Comedian Changed the Way I Preach

One of my favorite comedians is Pete Holmes. He became a favorite of mine, not because I love his standup (although it's brilliantly silly), but because I love his podcast. You Made It Weird is his avenue to interview people he loves and admires about art, creativity, sex, science, and God.

He's a believer in the sense that he loves to believe. He wants there to be a God, a mystery, and an afterlife. He wants to believe in more. This really comes out in his podcast. It's especially brilliant when he interviews his atheist comedian friends. These people are brilliant and they know how to articulate their worldview. They really are modern-day philosophers. If you listen intently to standup comedy, you'll hear thoughtful examination about the world, the mind, and more. And you'll hear some fart jokes!

While attending a three-day workshop in LA, I was determined to see Pete live somewhere, somehow. Sure enough, he was going to be at a small showroom for alt-comics. He was clearly working on new material, and it was fun to watch his process. I sat front row. I laughed, hard. I love laughing. I'm a good audience member if you're a good performer.

The show was great. No time for meet and greet afterward, but I got what I wanted out of it. The next day at my workshop, the guy we all came to see said that after lunch we had a special guest coming in. You guessed it! Pete Holmes came in to sit and discuss communication and art. I was pumped. He even mentioned me from the night before to illustrate a point. I thought this was pretty cool (he also mentions me by name on his 300th episode of the podcast).

His contribution to the discussion was about audience interaction for communicators. He explained that as a comedian with a hostile or unengaged audience, you can do one of two things. First, you could turn on the audience, begin berating them, make fun of them, really get them worked up, and make yourself and maybe a few others laugh. Or, he said, you can invite them to believe what you think is funny is, in fact, funny. This requires a different posture and tone. Inviting people isn't about fighting people.

This is a novel idea for churches. We can't make people believe any-thing. The more we try the more insulting we become. But if we invite people into a conversation, into relationship, we can win their hearts. At this point we can begin inviting them to believe what we believe about God is true. And better yet we can help them discover God themselves!

This kind of welcoming is uncomfortable for many because it lacks control.

We've never done it that way

The church isn't the only organization that tightens a grip when they feel control slipping and unfamiliarity taking over, but it's the organization I've experienced the most, so I'll speak more intelligently coming from that angle. You may understand this principle at work in your organization or community. Either way, it exists everywhere.

In my opinion, the greatest problem with the American Christian church isn't what people believe, but how they behave. More specifically how leaders behave in relation to an ever-changing culture. When leaders who once experienced a successful movement now see their denomination or sect barely gaining influence, everyone else becomes the problem and must be stopped.

This is so dangerous.

The moment I hear a church leader say, "Well, we've never done it like that before" or "That's not how we did it in (name the decade)" or "That will never work because of _____" I just picture them raising tightly clasped fists in the air.

This posture is not conducive to inviting. It's all about fighting. They have moved from inviting people to believe what they believe to fighting with people about what they believe.

Have you ever had a knock-down, drag-out fight with your spouse or partner and left feeling like meaningful discourse just happened? No. Of course not. You were fighting, and winning meant everything, even more than that person. We'll talk more about that in a minute.

I have a vision of the American Christian church that includes groups of people being known as the most accepting, understanding, welcoming people in every community. I see gatherings of people that invite others to believe what they believe rather than fight about what they believe. One wins people, while the other alienates and isolates them.

Empty Tables, Empty Churches

Trends

An overwhelming amount of research is showing that people are walking away from church in a significant way. America isn't just moving into a "post-Christian" but rather an "un-Christian" culture at an unprecedented rate. The fastest growing religiously affiliated group in America are the religious "nones."

This group isn't necessarily atheist. They aren't vile, hard-hearted, wicked sinners. They are average, everyday, hardworking, educated people. They have simply walked away from what they see as unnecessary ties to the church. Maybe they have a religious past complete with church hurt. But many just don't see God and Jesus present in church-people and want something more. They believe they can find it somewhere else.

The temptation is to just write these people off and surround ourselves with those like us, who like us. This allows us to elevate our status with God and proclaim we are persecuted Christians in an unholy nation. Feels good to portray ourselves that way.

The fact is, God loves the "nones." Jesus died for them. And I'm compelled to invite them into relationship with me, my faith community, and Jesus. I believe it's the only way to turn the tides. Invite.

Something Is Dying

I sat across from a much wiser, experienced former pastor, questions ready. He told me to bring my best questions. Remember how I said that asking questions is an art form? Yeah, I'm not great at it. Not yet at least. He gave me the signal to "go" and I began my first question. "You know how church in America is dying...?"

He cut me off.

"What do you do?"

"I'm starting a church in downtown Las Vegas," I explained.

"Do you feel like what you're doing is dying?"

I was stumped. Where was he going? This wasn't even my question. I didn't even get to a question.

"No," I answered. "We're growing actually."

"Okay...so church isn't dying."

I was still confused at this point. As I carefully searched for my next words, he continued.

"Maybe there's an idea of church dying in America. And it should. But church isn't dying. There's people all over doing interesting, exciting things. Things that are growing and alive."

I couldn't help but feel small and energized at the same time. My perspective had to change. "Church is dying" isn't hopeful. "An idea of church is dying" creates an expectation of rebirth and resurrection for a Jesus follower. Jesus had to die to rise again, and maybe our idea of church and Christianity in America needs to do the same.

Just today I saw a tweet from a prominent pastor calling for a new Reformation of the church. But I know this pastor. He's stuck in the old Reformation. You know, The Reformation. From five hundred years ago. If you can't let that die, you'll never see something resurrected in its place.

Our idea of churches and tables may need to die so we can give new birth to new ideas about churches and tables and chairs and people and energy and relationships.

Something is dying. But that's not always bad. Not if your hope is in something that can never die. Not if your hope is in something and someone who raises the dead to new life!

So, if something is dying and another thing is resurrecting, let's discuss the space we are creating and inviting people into.

Let's Talk About Space

"This isn't the time or place to talk about this," she whispered as she pulled her husband close. He raised his voice. "Like HELL it's not." He pulled away from her and slid down on the train bench seat. "I think now is a perfect time to talk about how you really see our marriage!"

She cowered in her seat. Withdrawing from the conversation, she turned her back to him, embarrassed. The husband stood, exasperated. The news of his wife's latest session with their marriage counselor had cut him to the core. Things were worse than he imagined.

"Talk to me!"

"I can't," she expressed, still in a whisper. "That's the problem."

There was a tension in the air and everybody on the train could feel it. As the space between the couple expanded and contracted with every movement and word, the environment grew more and more uncomfortable. The passengers were mentally and emotionally disturbed. They had little information, but they had enough experience to know this was serious.

"I guess it's over then!" The husband continued to raise his voice. And then his wife responded with a practical solution that everyone on the train could agree on...

"Can we just talk about this at home?"

What is it, and what does that mean?

A dictionary definition of space is as simply complex as...

> a boundless, three-dimensional extent in which objects and events occur and have relative position and direction.

Ultimately, it's the area of nothingness between people, places, and things. I would even posit that it's the area between shared ideas as well.

The story I just shared had all kinds of space, and that space mattered. Space affected the entire train car. The space between words, emotions, people, and lovers set the mood and changed the environment for everyone present. That's why the suggestion for a change of time and place was so powerful. Maybe you've experienced this.

Space matters when discussing heavy, emotional, and meaningful things. People's relationship to each other and shared ideas needs to be appropriately distanced. When situations grow passionate, space matters even more. That's because we all have a psychological bent that becomes affected by our physical surroundings, personal space.

Personal space is the region surrounding a person which they regard as psychologically theirs.

Some of us need more personal space than others. Some aren't "huggy" right away, and unwarranted physical contact is uncomfortable because someone has crossed a psychological line. For others, the idea that you aren't in close proximity bothers them greatly. Psychologically their personal space is especially open to friends and possible friends. But when it comes to unfamiliarity, we all draw boundaries, and when they are breached, we feel it, see it, and react to it.

Proxemics is the study of the spatial requirements of humans and the effects of population density on behavior, communication, and social interaction.

The man who coined this term, Edward Hall, emphasized the use of space on interpersonal communication in his study. He writes about its impact on how people relate to each other and the world around them; not just their homes but even the community in which they live and interact with others.

Personal intimacy is distinguished by how close in proximity we are allowed to exist with another person. It's why rape is such an especially heinous violation. It breeches a psychological, emotional space at the deepest level. Sex is deeply intimate because of proximity. Our homes and living situations are intimate. The proximity of space allows us to see people as they really are. That roommate who snores excessively, doesn't mind nudity, and/or overshares can be annoying because of proximity and familiarity.

Space matters.

While we all understand personal space and the all-encompassing impact it has on us personally, I think we all too often don't consider it in others. There are boundaries that we cross mentally, emotionally, socially, et cetera on a regular basis when we present ideas to others who may disagree. And there may even be unknown, deep hurt associated with an idea you shared passionately.

When we don't consider others and the space in which they exist, there's a real danger of expanding into unwanted, psychological territory that forces them to uncomfortably contract. At this point, reaching them becomes improbable, and meaningful conversation impossible.

An Inviting Space for Meaningful Discourse

Bars aren't the most comfortable places in the world for me. My father's parents were alcoholics, and he didn't want that for our family. I'm glad he didn't. I'm glad he took a different path. I grew up with a "no drinking" mindset. But it went beyond alcoholism in the family to "the Bible says so." I don't want to get too deep into this discussion, but as I read and plainly interpret the Bible ...

> *Drinking alcohol is not expressly forbidden.*
>
> *Drunkenness is clearly and strongly forbidden.*
>
> *If your drinking causes a fellow Christian who struggles with alcohol to stumble, it's best not to drink.*

That being said, when I moved to downtown Las Vegas I recognized one thing quickly...people hang out at bars. Sure, there are coffee shops. There's a great park. But people hang out in bars. And there's a reason why. It's a socially comfortable space (as are coffee shops) to exchange ideas, relax, and connect.

As I sat with another, innovating local pastor, discussing our vision for church in downtown Las Vegas, he was reminded of something another pastor was doing. It wasn't necessarily "church" but it was a gathering of people. Pub Theology was created as a low-risk opportunity for people to meet at a bar, pub, or brewery and discuss life and faith. I loved this idea, so I researched it.

There were a couple of books written by the creator of Pub Theology, as well as a website. I connected to the website community and ordered the books as quickly as I could. Sure enough, this event had some crucial elements of our church vision. I loved this idea. It fit Las Vegas. We had to try it.

I contacted the owners of a downtown Las Vegas brewery and, while they were hesitant, they agreed to let us host our first ever Pub Theology discussion group on a Monday night. Monday is kind of like a weekend for many people in our city. It was a great night for us! We promoted through social media and fliers. I had no idea what would happen. But at best it seemed as though we would have about six people. This was awesome!

I showed up early, pulled tables together, and ordered a Not Your Father's Root Beer. Yeah, I don't like beer. I sat quietly, nervously awaiting my fellow conversationalists. People started to show up. And then more came. I was shocked to see some friends from my former church. Then a group came in I didn't recognize. Then a few showed up I had invited personally. I couldn't believe they all came.

We had eighteen people that first night. Some identified as Christians, others as atheist, and still others as irreligious and unsure. It was a diverse group. We had a man from France, a casino host, one guy with cerebral palsy, the CEO of an event planning company, and even another DTLV pastor. We had to break up into two tables. And each table had its own personality. Conversation was meaningful. It went longer than the designated hour. Some people hung out for another hour talking and connecting.

I walked home down a quiet Fremont Street thinking...

Thank you, God!

People showed up!

I think this works!

Our church could look like this and it could be amazing!

Space to consider...

When creating space to have meaningful conversation about things like life and faith, we must first consider the space people may need to even begin having those conversations. Whether it's a neighbor we want to get to know better, a coworker with whom we starkly disagree, or a new friend we want to know exactly what we believe, it's important to consider them as we discuss important matters.

I think there's specifically five areas every person needs space to discuss life and faith...

Physical

Mental

Emotional

Social

Spiritual

Physical space sets the stage...

We did a survey recently through our friends at Wedgies, an online polling site. It was a simple, one-question poll. We wanted to know what type of environment (physical space) was ideal for people to discuss important matters. The choices were...

Living Room / Dining Room (Home)

Bar / Coffee Shop / Restaurant

Classroom

Meeting Room / Conference Room

Theater / Concert

Go ahead...answer for yourself.

The number two answer in this poll was a tie between Meeting/Conference Room and Bar/Coffee Shop/Restaurant. I was a little surprised with this response. But it certainly brought to light a few things about physical spaces. The top answer was probably what you said, Living/Dining Room. People find a home environment an ideal physical space to discuss things like life and faith.

This may be no surprise to people already connected to a church. Most churches have, at some level, home groups that meet throughout the week. In this setting many people connect relationally and spiritually. Some churches use phrases like "circles are better than rows" and "better together" and "get connected." This leveraging of homes is rooted in what the Bible tells us about the first Christians...

> "They worshiped together at the Temple each day, met in homes for the Lord's Supper, and shared their meals with great joy and generosity..."
>
> —Acts 2:46

There's something about the feel of a home. Not just your own home. Sure, that's where you're most comfortable. But even someone else's home can be oddly disarming. Couches are nice. Every home has that "comfy" chair. And sitting around a dinner table inspires all kinds of great conversation.

Think about that next, difficult conversation or meaningful discussion you need to have. The setting will matter. Consider the space in which you're bringing that person.

Now, if you're already in relationship with the people with whom you're having these important conversations, homes are probably ideal on several levels. But what if you want to connect with a community of people you may not know well? What if you want to share ideas and have people discuss them together, knowing they will disagree?

In these situations, I can't help but imagine that a neutral setting like a bar/coffee shop/restaurant is best. But what if you could combine familiar physical spaces into a new, very intriguing space that considers all of the friends, family, and strangers you want to discuss meaningful matters? We'll talk further about this in just a minute.

I think we can all agree, environment matters, and the physical space should match the desired relational outcome!

Mental space sets the mood...

There's a direct connection between physical and mental space. Our environment affects our mentality. Knowing what you want to talk about and the level of discourse desired will help you choose a physical space, but the time of day, day of the week, and even the mood of each party will either enhance or detract from everyone's ability to mentally engage in conversation.

If you want my mental best, there's a time to get it. You're probably the same.

These choices help others engage or disengage with discussion. Sometimes you can't really help the mental space someone is carrying with them to your conversation. But you can certainly help create space mentally for people to move from one state of mind to another. Humor helps. Genuine concern connects. Even tone of voice and well-crafted words can move your counterpart into productive discourse.

Whether you're teaching a class, leading a discussion group, having church, meeting an employee, or growing in friendship, it's important to mentally prepare yourself and others by considering factors that distract and engage.

Social space creates connectivity...

Certainly with close friends, but even more importantly with others, the social setting matters. Can people be themselves and be friendly in the space created? When discussing important matters there's always a tendency to grow passionate and create an "us versus them" gap in the conversation. This can be avoided if everyone understands this is supposed to be fun.

Sure, not all matters discussed regarding life and faith are light and fun. But even the heavy can be packaged in something fun. I heard one author/speaker call it "light, heavy, light." Can people have fun talking to you about what you believe? If you need to get heavy, get light first.

We've all heard of the compliment sandwich. Maybe you call it some-thing different, but you know what I mean. You need to bring in an employee who just isn't cutting it and discuss options. Every good leader starts by easing the situation with a compliment or positive connection socially. Then they move to the correction. Then they finish it off with another connecting point. Light, heavy, light.

This formula is great for creating social space in which people can discuss heavy things and leave friends and friendly.

Emotional space creates authenticity...

Let's face it...we've all got baggage. Relational luggage, backpacks full of past experiences, and a few carry-ons of assumptions weigh us down emotionally. Our education, family, passions, perspectives, and pasts affect the way we enter any and every conversation. Emotionally, we bring a lot to the table.

We all know this about ourselves and others, but it's not often considered when broaching meaningful conversations. Sometimes people need permission to hear something that hurts and hurt. Sometimes people need permission to set their luggage down and laugh. Other times people need their baggage identified, discussed, and carried by someone else for a bit. Some conversations are just more difficult because of our baggage.

Too many times we shy away from our emotions and the emotions of others. If we know they might get offended, or are passionate about something, we retreat from that subject. But what if we went right in to the heart of those matters as we build relationships through discussion? What if we gave people a warning that that's where we're going? That way they know which piece of luggage they should bring with them and which to set down.

Conversations are a journey. Some journeys require a lot of baggage and some don't. The path to authentic discussion is paved with emotional recognition. Not just ours, but theirs.

Spiritual space allows for diversity...

We are all on a spiritual journey of some sort because we are spiritual beings. Even if you don't believe in spirit and only embrace material, there are certain things that just scream spirit: love, beauty, intimacy, passion, purpose. They go beyond this material world. The problem some people get into is viewing everyone as on the same type of spiritual journey that they are traveling.

I had a theological discussion with a guy one time who just couldn't wrap his mind around how I reconciled two seemingly opposing theological ideas. Then I listened deeper. Most all of his argument for one side revolved around his experience. It had to be a certain way universally, because it was that way personally. But we all know that's not truth.

Spirituality is something we all experience, yet we all experience it differently. My story and experiences were opposite of his. And he didn't necessarily want to hear about my experiences because he had his own. This position tends to diminish the beauty of spiritual journey and mystery.

Every time I leave a Pub Theology discussion, I feel one thing so deeply. I feel that God is doing an amazing work in and around every person there. Now, I don't know exactly how their individual journeys will end, but I can clearly see everyone is on one. I'm excited every time. I appreciate that diversity.

But what if the spiritual space created doesn't embrace that spiritual authenticity and diversity? What if people don't feel like you love them because they are on a different journey? What if the spiritual space around you is so suffocating, there's just no room to be different from you?

Spiritual space matters because it acknowledges that there's an important diversity found in the journey. People should know they belong with you even if they don't believe like you, no matter what you believe!

Rethinking Church In Light Of Creating Space

One of the things you get to do when starting a church from the ground up is "rethink" what you do and why you do it. Now, there are certain things that cannot be recreated. But with everything else, I say dream, believe, and create. Along with my thoughts about the space necessary to discuss important matters with people who disagree, I began to imagine what church looked like with a little more conversation.

Vision

Simply put, the vision for Downtown Faith, our startup church in Downtown Las Vegas, is as follows...

> "*Creating space to discuss* life and faith."

Discussion matters to us, and creating the ideal space for these discussions is how we want to accomplish our mission of helping people follow Jesus. We believe that a lot of people have fewer problems with Jesus than they do with the church or organized religion. And a lot of that is because they don't feel heard by the church. We want to change that.

Our vision includes providing space in every gathering or service to discuss the ideas presented in the message, talk, sermon, or whatever you want to call it. We believe people are discussing spiritual matters; they just aren't discussing them with the church. There should be no safer, better place to discuss matters of life and faith than a church that follows Jesus, because there was no one better at discussing these matters with people than Jesus himself.

Why this vision? Jesus.

Jesus had great answers to questions about life and faith. Many times he diverted certain questions into better questions that got to the heart of the initial question. Jesus had spiritual discussions with people...

walking down the road.

getting water from a local well.

in the synagogues.

at night on rooftops.

at parties with society's worst, most hated groups.

in homes of unexpected hosts.

by camp fire, over dinner, and on boats.

around tables.

Jesus understood that physical space mattered and would often use the surroundings to illustrate a teaching. He would talk about being connected to him like he was a vine, all while walking by a vineyard. He discussed the rooms he would build to create a place for his disciples while walking by city apartment buildings. He even referred to himself as "Living Water" while talking to the woman at the well.

Jesus also grasped the importance of other spaces. He eased the emotional trauma felt by the woman caught in adultery and thrown at his feet for judgment. He understood the need for mental space while teaching about the true meaning behind Jewish law with Jewish people. He would tell them, "You have heard it said, but I say..." He also understood the social space necessary to discuss hard things, so he talked about his death over dinner with his disciples.

Why would we consider creating space for people to have these discussions? Because we believe Jesus considered the environment in every way possible when he engaged people in need of his help, love, and spiritual guidance.

Creativity in creating space...

The phrase above, "creating space," has permeated my heart and mind for months now. Since the first moment it became clear this was the vision for the church, I've been bombarded with practical application, teaching, and examples of what it truly means. I'd like to take some time to help you understand and maybe even take to heart the art of "creating space."

5 Spaces to Create That Could Help the Church Discuss Life and Faith:

1.) Spiritual Space: Any church who wants to encourage meaningful discourse with a diverse group of people must, first and foremost, create space for people spiritually. Most religious people cringe at the idea of sharing thoughts and asking questions about faith with people who don't believe like they do. Maybe they feel unprepared to do so (mostly on the misconception they need to "win" an argument) or maybe it's as simple as an insecurity about the strength of their faith.

But I believe the church should be the safest, most welcoming place in the world to ask questions, struggle with doubt, and have truly meaningful conversation about faith. Studies show that people are talking about what they believe and why. They just aren't talking about it with pastors and the church. This must change if the church is to reach people with a message of love and grace.

2.) Physical Space: As the core team grew for Downtown Faith, we began by having the specific discussion about what our environments for church gatherings should look and feel like if we want people to discuss faith and feel heard. The physical space itself has enormous potential to draw people in to discussion. A few things really stuck in everyone's mind:

No stage. There must be a removal from anything separating the speaker sharing ideas, and the people who will be discussing those ideas.

Level seating. Theater and stadium seating is out. Most people agree that a home or coffee shop feel is best to connect people to each other in conversation. Both of these settings provide comfortable, level seating.

In the round: Another aspect of engaging people is to present every-thing in a way that people are looking at each other eye to eye. This is important in creating meaningful discussion.

3.) Emotional Space: Everyone's got baggage. And let's be honest, very few people have neutral feelings toward religion and religious settings. Things must be presented with an emotional understanding of the current culture regarding matters of faith. It's not about what is said but rather how it is said that creates emotional space for people to be heard. Everyone must agree to be respectful, open, and attentive.

4.) Mental/Rational Space: I'm not sure why it seems crazy to "church people" that "unchurched" people find many things at church, in the Bible, and about God irrational. If we're honest, there are more than enough stories in the Bible that could have "rational" holes poked in them. Creating mental space means acknowledging these things up front and addressing them rationally. It really catches certain people off guard when people of faith recognize the supernatural as just that.

5.) Social Space: The idea, in any culture at any time, that the church is a hateful, judgmental group should be insane to any Christian. But it happens. Just listen. And most accusations are warranted. It shouldn't be this way. People who have been forgiven, shown grace and mercy, and loved as a Christian should be the most understanding, gracious, and loving people on the planet. Don't tell me how much you "love the sinner but hate the sin" until you've first loved the sinner well. Socially, the church should be well spoken of and appreciated for their influence in the community. I love when I see this!

For a church to create space in these ways, each person must create space in their heart first. A welcoming, inviting space for the "other." A seat at the table!

CHAPTER TEN

Fourth & Final Leg: Conversation

Moving From Monologue to Dialogue

> *A conversation is a dialogue, not a monologue.*
> *That's why there are so few good conversations:*
> *due to scarcity, two intelligent talkers seldom meet.*
>
> —Truman Capote

Shift in Culture

You've probably heard a politician, pastor, or protester say something about the importance of having a conversation. Maybe I notice it a lot more now that I truly believe in it, but I think culture is at least moving in that direction. The problem is people like this don't really mean it. As soon as someone in the conversation shares an idea or belief that's controversial, unpopular, or divisive, the whole thing crumbles. We need "safe spaces" on college campuses to shield us from ideas contrary to our own.

We tend to want our ideas shared and shouted from the rooftops, but there's little room for people to challenge them. Even a genuine question causes us to be defensive. This applies to all kinds of people, but I think church leaders and church people are the worst. Maybe they want to be like Jesus and have meaningful conversation, but it's just too difficult.

If you're reading this, you've probably been to church recently. How much dialogue happened? How much did you want to have? How many times during the pastor's talk did you have a question go unanswered? How often did you want to express doubt or disagreement?

I bet it's happened a lot. Unfortunately, there's just no room for doubt and questions and challenges and disagreements at your typical church. I think it's because there's a lack of tables. Podiums and stages and lights and pews and rows and "stand up" and "sit down" and "shake hands" doesn't really leave room for authentic, meaningful conversation.

When we first began the journey of starting a church for downtown Las Vegas, I sought out a video producer to create an engaging video for our website and fund-raising. I knew of a friend of a friend and reached out. I was told she probably wouldn't do it because it was for a church. This piqued my interest. I had to hear the story.

She wanted to hear our story too, so we met for coffee. I asked my questions and listened intently. She shared her religious background. A big important man with a big important book on a big important stage in a big important building was how she described the church. No place to ask questions and get answers. No place for disagreement. And no place for her as a woman. This is how she felt.

Our conversation helped her so much, she not only agreed to shoot our video—and it was awesome—she did it for free. She told us to consider her our first supporter. Why would a woman who felt alienated from and angry at the church and Christians agree to do that? I can only think it's because we had a real conversation. She felt listened to. She asked her questions and heard mine. We shared. Oh, and we were sitting at a table the whole time. I wasn't on a big stage with a big book. She wasn't in a pew. We were people. Human beings sitting across from one another and having a conversation about things that mattered.

Culture is shifting. People want to hear *and* be heard. They are thinking about things that matter. They are intelligent and articulate. Information is at their fingertips like never before. People need a place to filter and wrestle with that information. They need a place to grow and transform. They need Jesus. And they need the church of Jesus. Just not church as usual. They need the body of Christ to have better ears than ever before.

People need tables and chairs and other people and conversation and energy and relationship and an invitation.

TED Talks Meet Table Talk

There's a practical side to all of this conversation stuff as it relates to the church. I'm not saying we've got it all figured out, but we have created a space to teach people and provide opportunity to discuss life's most important matters. We call it "TED Talks Meet Table Talk."

This idea came to me after a conversation with a local high school principal. He is a man of integrity, intellect, passion, impressive leadership, and he loves Jesus. We started talking one night about teaching and learning. He told me that recent educational studies are showing a change in the way human beings learn. Here's how he explained it…

"The one talking is the one learning."

This rocked my world. I like talking and teaching. But none of it matters if people aren't learning. We all know that pastor who loves to hear himself talk. We don't learn a ton, but he's having fun. I had to avoid this. I had to leverage what we know about people and education to help people learn from Jesus. I had to get people talking. But I also had to talk in a way that would get them talking.

Then I came across TED. I know, late to the game really. According to its website...

> TED is a nonpartisan nonprofit devoted to spreading ideas, usually in the form of short, powerful talks.

Short, powerful talks. Spreading ideas. What if faith gatherings were devoted to spreading ideas in the form of short, powerful talks? What if those ideas came from the Bible? What if these ideas were worth discussing? What if they contained teachings of Jesus about love and happiness and newness and transformation and sin and generosity and community and God and more?

These were the questions I began to ask. I was becoming committed to conversation. This was the formula for the community in downtown I was coming to know better and better. People wanted this. Conversation is missing in society. That's a problem. We were going to help solve that problem. We were going to start conversations.

These conversations began happening and not without some struggle. People ingrained in a certain way of thinking and doing church were discussing faith with other people who didn't believe the same way. At church. This was difficult. Listening to someone deny Jesus while at church was a new idea. Some took real offense. It wasn't for them. But you know who was staying? The person who didn't believe in Jesus. Why? Because it was a safe place to have that conversation.

Conversation is the way forward. It may be the more difficult path, but it's undeniably key to reaching people. In her book, Reclaiming Conversation: The Power of Talk in a Digital Age, Sherry Turkle says this about the importance and healing power of conversation...

> "Conversation is on the path toward the experience of intimacy, community, and communion. Reclaiming conversation is a step toward reclaiming our most fundamental human values."

If people feel heard, they will engage. They will participate. They will come back. And through meaningful conversation they may, just may begin to follow Jesus. By sitting at our tables, they move toward the table of Jesus. And isn't that the point of all of this anyways?

CHAPTER ELEVEN

Final Thoughts

When you have more than you need,
build a longer table, not a higher fence.

—Unknown

There's a few more things I want to encourage you to think about as you continue your journey of table building. It's just that. A journey. It's not a journey of destination as much as a journey of transformation. It is a journey of rethinking our world, our theology, our neighbor, and more. There will be some cuts and bruises along the way. You may even lose a friend or two. Someone might call you a heretic. Remain humbly confident that God is opening you up to something more.

God's table isn't small. There are a lot of seats. Room enough for everyone. As we participate in building a bigger table, we must evaluate whether we are an obstacle to the invitation or a catalyst for conversation. Participation may require you to leave one tribe and find another. You may even have to start your own. But you'll never be as alone as you feel. There are people out there writing and working and speaking and loving and building bigger tables.

Keep learning. Find those people who can help you craft your table. Go find other tables and learn what you can.

The path to adulthood seems to be guided by teachers. Kids are learning so much all the time. It seems that everything and everyone is a teacher. Sometimes this is overt, as in a school or class setting. Other times our teachers are subtle. They could be a random neighbor with whom we engage sporadically, or a television show we love to watch.

I think of this often as I watch my kids. The first time my son counted to ten wasn't because of his mother or me. It was because *Mickey Mouse Clubhouse* had done activity after activity that counted to ten. I was shocked. My son knew this truth, but he didn't get it from me. As I'm writing this I know that this month he will begin preschool. I will entrust more learning to other people. People I don't really know.

As adults we tend to believe we have all of our thinking completely shaped. We aren't forced to learn institutionally, so we believe we aren't learning at all. But we are. At least we should be. I think we tend to follow the same path as children. It's just a little slower. Our brains are different. But that doesn't mean learning has stopped, and certainly it should not. As we grow up learning opposing ideas and shaping our personal beliefs, we tend to gravitate to certain teachers and preachers.

The closer we get to settling on our beliefs, the more we learn to filter the information we receive.

The filter we use is all too often one of comfort, familiarity, and agreement. But the times we learn best are those times we struggle with truly understanding what we believe and why. And struggle rarely happens in comfort, familiarity, and agreement. Understanding requires friction. Owning your path happens when you've worked to clear that path yourself.

3 People Who People of Faith Need

Faith is not lived in a bubble. The world is full of voices, information, teachers, and opinions. We can't get away. When people pursue spirituality, religion, faith, or anything greater than themselves, they will undoubtedly...

be taught by teachers.

face challenges and doubts.

think deeper about their beliefs in times of trial.

Even if we pretend we have it all figured out, there is no faith without doubt. They are partners, not enemies. Faith involves an element of not knowing, and that scares us all. We need people, the right people, to help inform our journey and discovery.

Have you ever felt afraid to tell someone at your church, "I just don't know if I believe it all"? Or maybe you've been caught in an intellectual conversation that belittles what you do think you know. Maybe you lie awake at night questioning everything from reality to existence. You feel isolated, afraid, and unable to move forward.

Fortunately, you aren't alone. You aren't isolated. And there is freedom in asking questions and admitting doubt. There's comfort in knowing others are searching and there is solid foundation in understanding the journey you're facing. As I continue to research what people are talking about, I find myself running to three types of people who I need as I grow and transform into everything God has for me.

Teachers Who Inform My Faith

If you're like me you have "chosen" a religion, faith, church, et cetera. You have a path and you're following it. For me, I follow Jesus. But within that tribe there are sub-tribes with all types of teachings on Jesus and life and faith and the Bible. I have narrowed my consumption of teaching to a few people who I have found…

have a solid grasp of how best to handle the Bible.

communicate clearly in a way I can understand truth best.

challenge me intellectually in my beliefs.

I need these people. I read their books, listen to their podcasts, and attend their talks about Jesus. These men and women help me grow in knowledge and faith. I need to hear their stories. I need to learn from their mistakes. I have these people in my life to inform what I believe about God, the Bible, and Jesus.

Here is a list of some of my favorites:

Andy Stanley, pastor, author, speaker, and leadership podcaster

A.W. Tozer, pastor, theologian, author from early 1900s

Tim Keller, pastor, author, and theologian

Bruxy Cavey, pastor, author, theologian

Skeptics Who Challenge My Beliefs

If our faith is never challenged, it is never completely owned. I grew up in church in the South. Pretty much everyone in my circle believed like I did, or at least they said they did. It was in college while working jobs with people who knew little or nothing of what I believed that I began to own my faith and live it more passionately.

Insecure people are afraid of challenge. They are the ones who bottle their kids up rather than letting them discover faith right alongside the other discoveries they are making about themselves and others.

Understanding that faith is attached to doubt removes that insecurity because you begin trusting the control of something bigger. One must discern truth and error while being challenged, but a little invited pushback is good for the soul.

Here is a couple of podcasts I invite to push back in areas of faith:

Pete Holmes, comedian, writer, spiritualist, and podcaster

Deconstructionist Podcast

Thinkers Who Stretch My Perspective

This group is the most interesting to me. It seems like these people spend time just being smarter than I am. They are philosophers, spiritualists, or pastors who see the world, faith, religion, and God differently from me. They may or may not be part of my "tribe" of faith. They might be in one of those hundreds of sub-tribes.

These "thinkers," as I'll call them, are passionate about this thing that is greater than they are from which everything flows, but they aren't always consistent on what they call that thing. Many times their faith is broad. People like Jesus and Buddha are of the same ilk. Terms like "God" can be used to describe this bigger thing, but it's only one of many. They meditate, pursue social justice, speak to thousands or even millions, and they truly live what they believe.

I enjoy finding intersecting points of faith as I listen to this group. They help me reconcile my limited views on...

an unavoidable God who just doesn't fit in my box.

other people who have given their life to pursue faith.

the thinking of people in this vast world.

Here is a list of a few "thinkers" I let challenge me:

Rob Bell, author, spiritual adviser, speaker, and podcaster

Father Richard Rohr, spiritual director, author, and speaker

Alexander Shaia, author, speaker, spiritual teacher

Peter Rollins, philosopher, theologian, author, and speaker

I know what some of you are thinking. It's okay. I haven't gone off the deep end. If anything, I've tasted and seen and cannot untaste or unsee. These lists could be longer and I'm always looking for new teachers and skeptics to help me grow. I want to encourage you to do the same.

The byproduct of expanding my understanding of God and the gospel is a bigger, more welcoming table with chairs and people and energy!

CPSIA information can be obtained
at www.ICGtesting.com
Printed in the USA
BVHW091444200519
548791BV00006B/625/P

9 781478 797548